FIRM FOUNDATIONS

TECHNIQUES AND QUILT BLOCKS FOR PRECISION PIECING

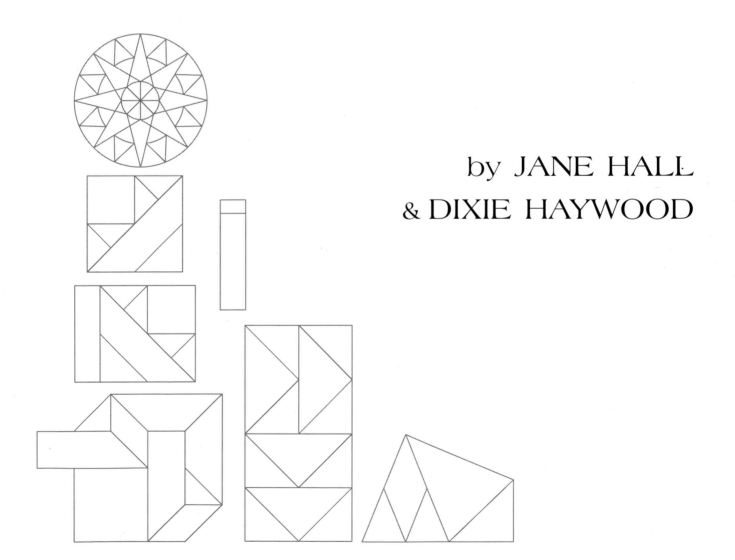

by JANE HALL
& DIXIE HAYWOOD

DEDICATION

We dedicate this book to the next generation of quilt lovers.

Morgan Elizabeth Rehrig, Graham Neil Rehrig, Matthew Donald Hall,
Emma Hall Kessel, and Patrick Hall Champagne.

Tyler Lewis Haywood, Cedar Lewis Howard, and Raven Forrest Howard.

Black & White photographs by Robert M. Hall and Robert C. Haywood
Color photographs by Charley Lynch, except as noted.

Located in Paducah, Kentucky, the American Quilter's Society (AQS), is dedicated to promoting the accomplishments of today's quilters. Through its publications and events, AQS strives to honor today's quiltmakers and their work – and inspire future creativity and innovation in quiltmaking.

Library of Congress Cataloging-in-Publication Data

Hall, Jane
 Firm Foundations: techniques and quilt blocks for precision piecing
/ Jane Hall & Dixie Haywood
 p. cm.
 Includes bibliographical references (p. 130).
 ISBN 0-89145-867-0
 1. Patchwork--Patterns. 2. Patchwork quilts. I. Haywood, Dixie.
II. Title.
 TT835.H3319   1996   96-1761
 746.9'7–dc20   CIP

Additional copies of this book may be ordered from: American Quilter's Society,
P.O. Box 3290, Paducah, KY 42002-3290 @ $18.95. Add $2.00 for postage & handling.

Printed in the U.S.A. by Image Graphics

CONTENTS

PREFACE

Precision Pieced Quilts Using the Foundation Method, our last book, was conceived as a comprehensive survey of all the methods that could be used for piecing on foundations. We explored past and present usage of design categories traditionally worked on foundations and noted contemporary uses of foundations in innovative work. We took foundation work a step further by introducing concepts that allowed the use of foundations for patterns not previously done on foundations. It was both a pattern and a design book, and we thought it was the last word on this old-made-new technique.

When we proposed Precision Pieced Quilts, we were told there was no demand for a book on this technique. We hope you don't mind if we laugh all the way to the quilt shows, where quilts made with foundations are garnering awards; to the classroom, where quilters are thrilled to learn methods that will make their quilting easier and more creative; and to the bookshops, where several good books have followed our lead.

Why another book on foundation piecing? As we use foundations to make our own quilts, we have discovered more techniques we want to share. As we travel and teach, we discover that when quilters who are exposed to the initial concept realize the tremendous advantages of working on a base, they begin to experiment and come up with even more ways to utilize this method.

We believe foundation piecing is at the point quick-piecing and no-template cutting were ten years ago, growing exponentially. The tremendous popularity of pre-stamped patterns on muslin and paper, the spate of articles on foundation piecing, as well as the enthusiasm with which we have been greeted as we teach only reinforces this conviction.

This book provides larger-sized traditional block patterns not usually seen for foundation piecing. We believe it will be useful to quilters at all levels who seek more accurate piecing techniques. If you are familiar with foundation piecing, we hope this book will expand your repertoire. If you are not familiar with it, prepare to learn new ways to work and play. Our hope is that you will find the blocks we show intriguing enough to work into quilts, and that they will challenge you to adapt this technique to your own uses.

No one person – or even two – can write a book without the help of many others. We thank all the quiltmakers, professional and amateur, who have encouraged us and who have shared their quilts and ideas. You will find their quilts throughout the book. We also thank Bernina of America for the loan of a sewing machine, and Easy Tear™ for supplying foundation material for many of our blocks. Books, patterns, and foundation supplies are listed in the Bibliography and Resource List.

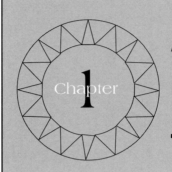

THE WHY OF
FOUNDATION PIECING

Chapter 1

Contemporary quiltmakers build on the past, but we don't necessarily create our designs with the same techniques our foremothers used. Foundations, a separate base on which to piece, have been used for generations to provide stability when working with difficult-to-control fabrics such as the silks, velvets, ties, and ribbons used in crazy quilts. Stabitlity was also needed when working with such patterns as Log Cabin and Pineapple (Fig. 1-1), where it is easy to skew the block as it builds around the center. Thrift, as well as stability, was a consideration as fabric was created by combining leftovers, often off-grain, in myriad versions of string quilts.

The contemporary quilter is building on time-honored, proven uses when she continues to use old forms such as strings, crazy patch, and the Log Cabin family of patterns with both traditional and more innovative applications. In addition to stability, however, today's quilters also turn to foundations for precision, speed, and design assistance, although not every element may be important on a given undertaking. In this chapter, we will explore how these advantages apply to different situations; in Chapter 2, we'll show you how to use foundations to realize these advantages.

DIFFICULT PATTERNS
Foundation piecing has an advantage over conventional piecing for difficult patterns because it enables quilters to work with patterns which they may have avoided until now. Foundations can provide stability and precision to patterns that are easily skewed or have many points that need to be matched. Mariners Compass (Fig. 1-2 and Block Plates 64, 65, 66) has both of these problems. Baby Bunting (Fig. 1-3) with its curves and points is another such pattern.

The Palm (Fig 1-4 and Block Plate 15) is a classic block more often seen in illustrations than in quilts, perhaps because of the daunting task of keeping all the points intact. Even the Eight

FIG. 1-1. ANTIQUE LOG CABIN BLOCKS

FIG. 1-2. MARINERS COMPASS

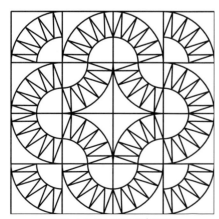

FIG. 1-3. BABY BUNTING

Pointed Star (Fig. 1-5 and Block Plate 45) with center points coming together and side and corner set-ins is, for many people, a difficult pattern.

Op-Art designs, with graphics created by strong value contrasts, fascinate many quilters (Fig. 1-6). The precision required to achieve the exact joins that makes them effective puts them in the "someday" drawer. And we can't resist mentioning one of our favorite patterns, Pineapple (Fig 1-7 and Block Plates 10, 11), as an example. With its center-out piecing and eight-plane design, it is easily distorted if care is not taken in its construction.

Not only can foundations ensure stability and precision for these difficult types of blocks, but they also will give a quilter the confidence to attempt them. This opens a whole new world of patterns that many think are far beyond their capability because of complexity or degree of difficulty.

SIMPLE PATTERNS WITH DIFFICULT ELEMENTS

Quilters are discovering that foundations can be used to simplify the piecing of difficult elements within a block that in itself doesn't appear especially complicated or advanced. While the difference between "difficult patterns" and "simple patterns with difficult elements" may seem academic, in this category we include the 54-40-or-Fight Star (Fig. 1-8) and even the ubiquitous Flying Geese

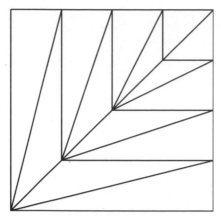

FIG. 1-4. THE PALM

FIG. 1-6. OP-ART DESIGN

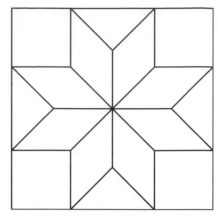

FIG. 1-5. EIGHT POINTED STAR

FIG. 1-7. PINEAPPLE: FOUR BLOCKS

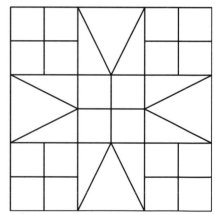

FIG. 1-8. 54-40-OR-FIGHT STAR

and its variations (Fig. 1-9). Foundations help to control and keep even simple points uniform.

Other examples of patterns with sharp angled corners, bias edges, and curves in a block with otherwise simple piecing, include Dogwood Blossoms (Fig. 1-10) or Thorny Thicket (Fig. 1-11). It is not necessary to piece an entire block on a foundation to benefit from its advantages. Foundations can be combined with conventional piecing in the same block.

GROUP QUILTS

Quilters love block exchanges, round robins, block-of-the-month raffles, and making group quilts of all kinds: friendship quilts,

charity quilts, and raffle quilts. If blocks are to be pieced by a group, foundations guarantee that the blocks will all be the same size. A common complaint with group quilts of any kind has been the wide disparity in size of the incoming blocks. Guaranteed uniformity is a dream come true for group quilt efforts.

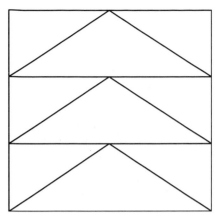

FIG. 1-9. FLYING GEESE

FIG. 1-10. DOGWOOD BLOSSOMS

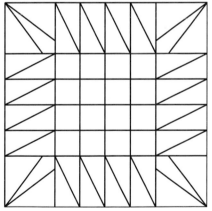

FIG. 1-11. THORNY THICKET

Because friendship blocks are so popular, we have included five blocks especially suitable for signatures in the pattern section. There are also three group quilts in the Gallery (Gallery Plates 1, 2, 3).

BORDERS AND SASHES THAT FIT

Pieced borders and sashes can provide the finishing touch to a quilt. Even with painstaking measuring, cutting, and piecing, pieced borders are inherently unstable, a fact that causes many quilters to avoid them. Foundations can keep the border within bounds, making it fit perfectly. Using a foundation can make simple work of piecing and attaching a border and can open new vistas for border design. Many quilts in the Gallery show varying pieced border possibilities.

PATCHWORK FOR GARMENTS

As patchwork-embellished garments have gone from looking like "walking quilts" to sophisticated designer clothing, they have attracted interest from those whose skills in dressmaking are more advanced than their skills in patchwork. Foundations make patchwork accessible to them, as well as making clothing construction easier for the experienced quilter.

Foundations are invaluable when using difficult-to-handle fabrics, whether in the body of the garment or in added patchwork details. They also can provide a built-in lining or interlining for patchwork, making washing and pressing of patchwork areas easier.

Two vests and a jacket in the Gallery (Gallery Plates 10, 11, 12)

show the effectiveness and versatility of using foundations in wearable art.

DESIGN FUNCTIONS

Foundations have a great deal to offer both the quilter who designs original patterns and one who uses traditional patterns for innovative color or layout variations. The control foundations provide gives freedom to improvise, makes difficult designs or colorations manageable, and helps avoid annoying mistakes in both planning and assembly.

Many contemporary quilters use foundations as a design aid for their work. After preliminary planning, an overall design such as Cynthia England's PIECE AND QUIET (Gallery Plate 37) or Eileen Sullivan's AFTER THE STORM (Gallery Plate 36) can be drawn directly onto a foundation, coding colors, fabric placement, and construction sequence.

Traditional block patterns with non-traditional coloration and innovative graphics can be very confusing to piece. By marking the colors directly on foundations, piecing can proceed easily. Many of our own quilts shown in the Gallery reflect this advantage.

The next two chapters will show you how to use foundation piecing in your own quiltmaking to benefit from any or all of these advantages.

Chapter 2

THE HOW OF
FOUNDATION PIECING

Foundation piecing involves a variety of options: in materials, in marking methods, and in piecing techniques. The choices may be dictated by the project you are making, by your preferences, or by a combination of the two.

MATERIALS

Before choosing the material for your foundation, you need to decide whether the foundation will be permanent or temporary. The chart on page 9 will give you a comparison of the chacteristics of the materials for both types of foundations.

•PERMANENT FOUNDATIONS

Permanent foundations are left in place for the life of the quilt. They are especially appropriate for clothing and decorator items such as pillows, table runners, tree skirts, and the like. They may be advisable for fabric that ravels or is lighter weight, both because the item will wear or hang better and because the fabric will not be stressed as the foundation is removed. Perma-

nent foundations work well with machine quilting and with quilts that are tied. They can be used with hand or machine piecing.

Material for permanent foundations includes fabric of all weights; non-woven interfacing except the all-bias variety; flannel; and, in some cases, fleece. Batting can be used in conjunction with a fabric backing for string or crazy piecing, but is not recommended where precision is required.

The weight of the material should vary depending on what you are making. For instance, to maintain the qualities of the fabric you are using for a garment, you might want a batiste foundation for silk. However, if you are making a pleated Log Cabin wall quilt of silk, non-woven interfacing would give the body needed to hang well. A muslin foundation works well for cotton, as does a flannel foundation when piecing with wool. These foundations may act as an interlining, with or without batting, or as the final lining.

Materials for permanent foundations require some care in handling and pressing. They should all be pre-shrunk before using. Foundations of woven fabric can be stretched if carelessly handled. To give such foundations more stability while piecing, spray them with fabric sizing or starch.

•TEMPORARY FOUNDATIONS

Temporary foundations are removed after the project is completed. They are ideal for anything that will be hand quilted, eliminating the extra layer a permanent foundation adds.

Materials for temporary foundations are usually paper, which is readily available in various weights and types. This includes tracing paper, letter-weight paper, freezer paper, and adhesive paper. We have recently discovered that the lightweight paper used on physicians' examining tables makes an excellent foundation material. Most types of paper including freezer paper are available with marked grids, which can be useful in keeping grainlines consistent or for matching points and lines when blocks are broken into segments.

Removable non-woven interfacing also makes a good temporary foundation. Easy-Tear™ is a new lightweight removable interfacing which has all the attributes of tracing paper, but is more durable and less likely to tear when handled.

For general use, we like to use temporary foundations that are as thin as possible, such as tracing paper or lightweight interfacing. They are easy to mark, to see fabric through, and to remove without stitch damage or fabric distortion. They reduce the bulk and weight of the quilt top under construction, especially on a large project. Because you can use a medium stitch length on thin foundations, errors can be corrected without destroying the foundation. Realize, however, that paper may tear with frequent handling. Rag-content tracing paper is the most stable and is least likely to tear prematurely. It is, of course, more expensive.

Freezer paper has special uses in piecing with difficult fabrics which are loosely woven, slippery, or cut on the bias. It also controls long slender points and makes possible tight joins with absolute precision. It is slightly more difficult to remove than tracing paper. Fabric can be "press-basted" in position to start a segment by touching it with the tip of a hot iron to secure it without ironing the whole segment (Fig. 2-1). This is the foundation of choice for many quilters because of the control it gives, especially at the edges of a block. A similar, but more expensive material, is adhesive-backed paper such as that used for shelf lining or name tags. It adheres better than freezer paper but will melt if ironed.

Sewing on temporary foundations is, with few exceptions,

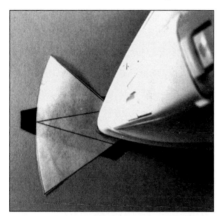

FIG. 2-1.

MATERIALS AT A GLANCE

PERMANENT FOUNDATIONS:

- **Batting** – Recommended only for string or crazy piecing. Must be used with fabric backing.
- **Fabric** – Match weight of fabric to project; pre-shrink.
- **Flannel** – Can hand quilt if used as combination foundation-filler; pre-shrink.
- **Fleece** – Should be used alone only with care against distortion; can be combined with a fabric
- **Non-woven interfacing** – Match weight to fabric or use; pre-shrink; use non-bias type backing.

TEMPORARY FOUNDATIONS:

- **Adhesive paper** – For use with single foundations; can be used with hand piecing; adheres well.
  Do not iron – melts with heat.
- **Examining table paper** – Lightweight and inexpensive; translucent; can tear out prematurely
- **Freezer paper** – Good for use with difficult-to-handle fabric. Use shiny side against fabric. Removal somewhat difficult when stitched on and pressed repeatedly; may lift prematurely with single foundation piecing or frequent handling.
- **Letter weight paper** – Use very small machine stitches; can distort loose stitch tension when removed; can tear out prematurely.
- **Removable interfacing** – use lightweight types. Less likely to tear prematurely than paper.
- **Tracing paper** – Fabric visible when *under* press-piecing. Rag paper less likely to tear prematurely.

done by machine. While non-woven interfacing can be used for hand piecing, removal is difficult and must be done with care to avoid breaking the stitches. The good news for those who usually sew by hand is that foundation piecing makes even a sewing machine novice a precision piecer.

It is important to sew on temporary foundations with small stitches so the piecing remains secure and the stitches tight when the added bulk of the foundation is removed. We like to use a size 70-80 needle and 12 – 16 stitches to the inch, depending on the fabric/foundation combination. On European machines, this is at the 1½ to 2 stitch setting. This is small enough to maintain the integrity of the stitch, but still makes it possible to take out stitching if necessary. However, if you stitch on letter-weight paper you need an even smaller stitch to compensate for the thickness of the paper and to keep from distorting the stitch tension.

MARKING TECHNIQUES

Foundations must be marked with the pattern to be pieced. They can also be marked with piecing order, color coding, and construction sequence of segmented designs. You can choose from a wide variety of marking tools and methods. Some choices depend on the foundation material you use, but many work with more than one material (Fig. 2-2).

FIG. 2-2. MARKING TOOLS

•BASTING

Basting, by hand or machine, can be used for marking guidelines. It is one of the few marking methods that is practical for fleece or batting.

•COMPUTER PRINTING

It is possible to print unlimited numbers of identical foundations using the computer's ability to design and print patterns. Many quilt design software programs have libraries of blocks which can be printed out, limited only by the size of the printer. Usually no distortion occurs, regardless of which type of printer is used – dot-matrix, ink-jet, or laser. Size may be limited by the capacity of your printer. In addition to the usual copy paper, which necessitates an extra-small stitch when piecing, you can put lighter weight paper, interfacing, freezer paper, and even fabric through a computer printer. To avoid wrinkling, you can press fabric onto freezer paper

MARKING AT A GLANCE						
TOOL	**BATTING**	**FABRIC**	**FLANNEL**	**FLEECE**	**INTERFACING**	**PAPER**
Basting	X	X	X	X	X	
Computer		X			X	X
Copy Machine		X		.	X	X
Hera	X	X	X	X		X
Hot-iron Transfer		X	X		X	
Needlepunching					X	X
Pre-Printed		X				X
Pencils and Pens	X	X	X	X	X	X
Stamps		X	X		X	X
Stencils		X	X	X	X	X
Tracing Wheel		X	X	X	X	X

to give it enough firmness to slide through the rollers of the printer.

•COPY MACHINE

This has become a popular method of reproducing patterns which, like computer printing, can result in duplicate foundations. We do not recommend the use of a copy machine for any repeat-block pattern. Every copy machine distorts to some extent, usually in one direction only. If you are making a large block on a good copy machine, the small inaccuracy may not be critical. If you are working in a smaller size, accurate assembly of the blocks will be difficult.

Copy machines can be useful for enlarging or printing foundations for pictorial or free-form designs, though lines at the edges of the block may need adjustment. Fabric, freezer paper, and interfacing can be fed into many of them. If you use a copy machine, it is important to print from the original to keep any distortion from being compounded.

•HERA

Hera is a Japanese tool with a fine edge, used to mark an impressed line directly on the fabric. It works with many types of foundations, temporary and permanent. It will tear paper if too much pressure is applied.

•HOT IRON TRANSFER

Hot iron transfers can be created using pencils made for that purpose. The pencils, available at quilt, hobby, and variety stores, are used to trace the pattern onto paper, which then can make multiple copies when ironed onto the foundation. Use rag-content paper to make the transfer so it will not be burned by the iron. The transfer can be re-marked and used again. Be sure to keep the pencil sharp; the soft lead dulls quickly. Check the tracing for accuracy before making copies.

•NEEDLEPUNCHING

This is our favorite method for marking paper foundations. It also can be used with non-woven interfacing although it is more difficult to see the punches, especially when *under* press-piecing with a light fabric. Up to twelve copies can be made at a time. Pin the pattern to be copied to a stack of paper and, starting in the middle of the pattern, run the pattern through an unthreaded sewing machine, stitching on each line (Fig. 2-3). After a line or two, the stack will be stuck together by the punched holes, and the finished stack of foundations will stay together until each is peeled off for use. Before removing the pattern, turn over the stack to be sure all lines have been marked.

A unique advantage of a punched foundation is that one side is smooth and the other is slightly rough where the needle pierced the paper. Placing the fabric on the rough side helps

FIG. 2-3.

hold the fabric patches as they are positioned and sewn.

•PRE-PRINTED FOUNDATIONS

A wide variety of pre-printed patterns on paper and fabric foundations are available from several companies. Instructions range from detailed to minimal. See Resource List.

•PENCILS AND PENS

We prefer to use a mechanical pencil with a fine lead when marking foundations, but any sharp pencil can be used. When marking fabric, use a cutting mat or sandpaper under the foundation to keep the pencil from dragging and distorting the fabric. Mark slowly and check for accuracy when you are finished. Using different colored pencils sometimes may help key a design to fabric or color placement.

Pens can be used if the marks are fine enough to not distort the pattern and permanent so the ink does not bleed onto the patchwork. Many of the quilt marking pens and pencils have thick tips and make accurate marking difficult.

•STAMPS

Several companies market stamps for marking foundations. For the most part, they are for small blocks and traditional patterns. You also can have them custom made at office supply companies. See Resource List.

•STENCILS

Pre-cut stencils can be used for marking foundations. Several companies make them for this purpose; you also can make them yourself. Use care that the pattern is not distorted as you draw, either by moving the stencil or by not being consistent about which edge of the cut you use. See Resource List.

•TRACING WHEEL

A tracing wheel can mark any foundation except batting. It can be used alone when marking paper, or with dressmaker carbon when marking fabric or interfacing. With layers of carbon paper, more than one foundation can be marked at a time.

PIECING TECHNIQUES

There are three major foundation piecing techniques: *top* pressed-piecing, *under* pressed-piecing, and single foundation piecing. There are also several hybrid techniques using foundations. All of these can be used alone, in combination with each other, and/or with conventional piecing.

Pressed-piecing is the method that comes to mind most immedi-

ately when thinking of foundation piecing. Pressed-piecing, sometimes called "sew and flip," is commonplace with such patterns as Log Cabin and Pineapple, string, and crazy quilting (Fig. 2-4). The last two are always pieced on a foundation, and Log Cabin and Pineapple blocks are often pieced that way. These techniques can be sewn by hand or machine depending on the foundations used. Because of our preference for temporary foundations, we most often piece by machine.

FIG. 2-4. TRADITIONAL
PRESS-PIECED BLOCKS

Pressed-piecing is done by positioning the first piece of fabric, either by pin or glue stick, with the wrong side against the foundation. The next piece is placed on top of the first, right sides together, and the two are stitched together, through the foundation. The second fabric is pressed open to the right side and, depending on the pattern, may be cut or trimmed before the next piece is added. Each piece of fabric in the pattern is added in the same manner, following the piecing order.

We divide the technique into two types: *top* and *under* pressed-piecing. The techniques are largely, but not entirely, interchangeable. The first is done by aligning the fabric on top of the foundation on fabric placement lines and stitching ¼" inside the lines. The second is pieced with the fabric placed under the foundation, sewing on lines marked on top of the foundation.

Which technique to use sometimes is determined by the pattern or the foundation, but most often is open to personal choice. Precision can be achieved with either technique, although the results may be more efficient or more consistent for a specific pattern with one or the other method. Random string piecing is probably faster pieced with *top* pressed-piecing; planned string piecing may be more accurate with *under* pressed-piecing.

Whichever method you use, pressing is an important part of the process. Results of pressing will be improved by using the dressmaker technique of "setting" the stitches. Do this by pressing the stitching line as sewn, before opening the added piece (Fig. 2-5). Then open and press the strip of fabric firmly against the seam from the fabric side. Check that you have not pressed in pleats or tucks; folds from careless pressing can create inaccurate points and joins. Press again from the foundation side. The fabric needs

FIG. 2-5.

to be taut against the foundation so the block does not "grow" when a temporary foundation is removed, or pucker on a permanent foundation.

We'll use a Courthouse Steps version of the Log Cabin block to illustrate both pressed-piecing methods (Fig. 2-6 and Block Plate 1). The numbers on the pattern indicate the piecing order. This block is traditionally pieced in two values; use light fabric for the odd-numbered patches and dark fabric for the even numbers.

Use either paper or fabric as a foundation. The bulk or stiffness of the foundation may seem cumbersome at first. If you roll the foundation to the area being

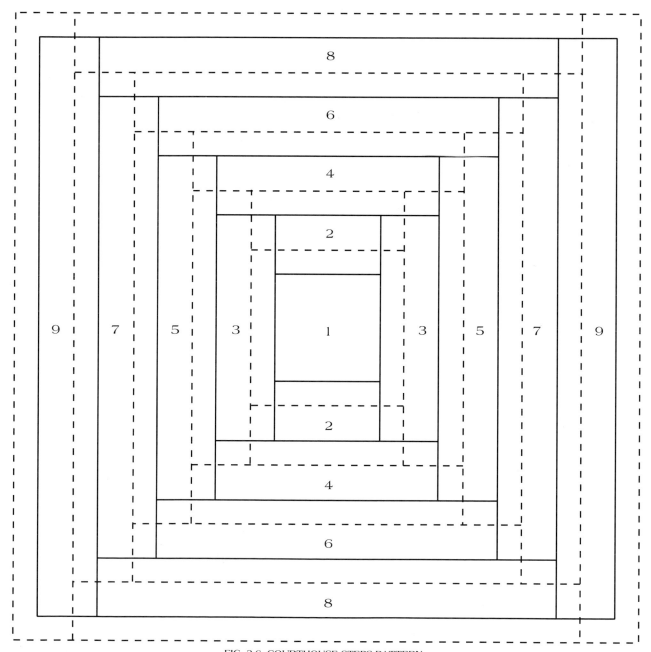

FIG. 2-6. COURTHOUSE STEPS PATTERN
Dashed lines are fabric placement lines;
solid lines are sewing lines.

13

pieced, not only will it be easier to handle, but also it will be less apt to crumple or tear (Fig. 2-7).

•TOP PRESSED-PIECING

Top pressed-piecing is initially easier to understand because we are used to sewing on fabric. It may be the choice of those with good machine sewing skills who can consistently sew ¼" seam allowances. Lynn Graves, inventor of the Little Foot™ that makes achieving a ¼" seam allowance easier, has built a pattern company geared to *top* pressed-piecing and shows that virtually any pattern that can be foundation pieced can be done with this technique.

It is easiest to achieve accuracy with *top* pressed-piecing if the distance from the edge of your presser foot to the needle is ¼". If it is not, you may be able to adjust the needle position to ¼". If this cannot be done, adjust the seam allowance to fit the measurement of your presser foot or, better yet, invest in a ¼" presser foot. In addition to the Little Foot™, many sewing machine companies have their own; Bernina's #37 foot is an example.

The following directions assume you are using a presser foot measuring ¼" from edge to needle (Fig. 2-8).

Prepare the foundation by tracing the dotted lines from the pattern

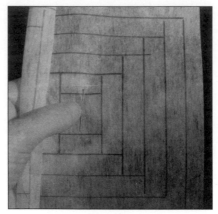
FIG. 2-7.

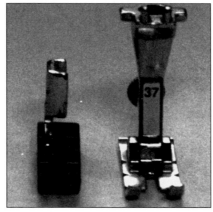
FIG. 2-8.

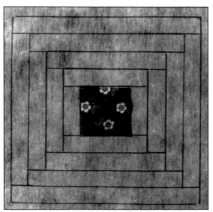
FIG. 2-9.

onto a foundation. Cut away any excess foundation a short distance from the outside line. The marked lines for *top* pressed-piecing are fabric placement lines. The fabric is laid along these lines and stitched ¼" inside them. The line will be your measuring line for stitching. It is important that fabric does not extend over the line and obscure it, as this affects the precision of the block.

Cut the center a scant 1¾" square, and one 1⅛" strip each of a dark and a light fabric. These measurements include ¼" seam allowance. Position the square right side up on the foundation within the center fabric placement lines, trimming if necessary to ensure that the lines are visible. Secure it with a pin or a dot of glue stick (Fig. 2-9). Lay a light strip for either patch #1 along one edge of the square, right side down. It is not necessary to pin the top strip.

Keep the edge of your presser foot along the drawn line and stitch with a ¼" seam allowance (Fig. 2-10). Open the strip and press. The outside edge of the strip should just meet the next fabric placement line (Fig. 2-11). If it is short of the line, you may have taken too large a seam; if it covers the line, you may have taken too narrow a seam. Adjust the strips and restitch if necessary.

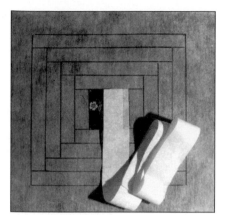

FIG. 2-10.

FIG. 2-11.

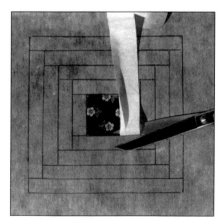

FIG. 2-12.

If the seam allowance is correct and the fabric does not meet the line, it may not have been cut accurately. This is not a problem unless the resulting seam allowance is too narrow to hold securely. In a block with many seams, this grading of the seam may be desirable to reduce bulk. However, it is important for the accuracy of the block that the next fabric sewn is aligned along the fabric placement line rather than along a skimpy seam allowance.

To cut the strip easily, lay the scissors on the strip with the blade open. Pull the fabric across the lower blade, sliding the scissors to the next line (Fig. 2-12). Cut so the line is visible and pin the strip to the foundation. Add another strip of the same fabric on the opposite side of the square, covering the second #1 patch (Fig. 2-13).

Using the same technique, sew strips of the darker fabric on the #2 patches (Fig. 2-14). Continue piecing, using the light strips for the odd numbered patches and dark for the even ones until the block is complete (Fig. 2-15).

The outer line on the foundation includes ¼" seam allowance for joining the blocks. You may turn the block over and machine baste with a long stitch just inside the edge of the foundation (Fig. 2-16).

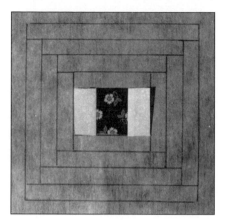

FIG. 2-13.

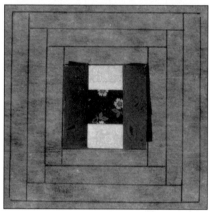

FIG. 2-14.

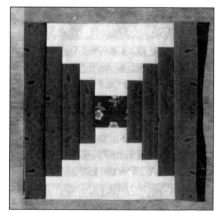

FIG. 2-15.

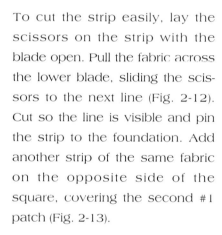

This will keep the fabric in place while the blocks are sewn together and the basting stitches will pull out easily as the foundation is removed.

To adapt any pattern to *top* pressed-piecing, draw fabric placement lines ¼" outside of each seam line (Fig 2-17).

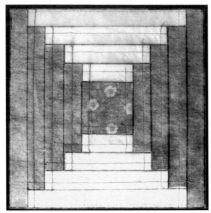

FIG. 2-16.

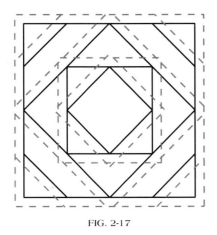

FIG. 2-17

•UNDER PRESSED-PIECING

Under pressed-piecing involves sewing directly on the foundation, with the fabric underneath. This is our method of choice when precise points are needed. It is also the technique for those who like to sew on a visible line. Although it takes a little practice to get used to having the fabric

largely out of sight under the foundation, and it may take more pinning, it is possible to achieve extremely accurate piecing without sewing an exact seam allowance. Being able to see the points and crossing joins makes matching seams easy, precise, and stress-free.

Prepare the foundation by tracing the solid lines from the pattern onto a foundation which is cut roughly ½" outside the final solid line. These lines are the sewing lines.

Cut a 1¾" center square and a 1⅛" strip each of light and dark fabric. These cuts include a ¼" seam allowance. Position the fabric square right side up on the undrawn side of the foundation, making certain the fabric covers the lines of the inner drawn square, with adequate seam allowances on all sides (Fig. 2-18).

Cut two pieces from the light fabric strip, each the length of a side of the center square. As with *top* pressed-piecing, lay the first piece along the edge of the center square at patch #1, with right sides together. Pin in place through all layers, making sure the pin is not near the sewing line (Fig. 2-19).

Turn the foundation over, and with the fabric underneath, against the feed dogs of the sewing machine, stitch through

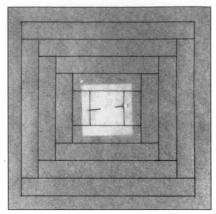

FIG. 2-18.

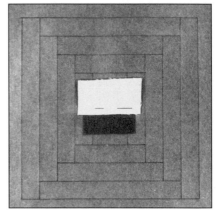

FIG. 2-19.

FIG. 2-20.

all layers (Fig. 2-20). Sew on the drawn line, beginning and ending two stitches beyond each end of the line (Fig. 2-21). These overrun stitches will be crossed and anchored by the next seam sewn, and do not need to be backstitched.

Open the strip just sewn, press, and pin it in place. It is helpful to pin directly in the seam allowance of the strip just sewn to flatten and hold the press. The pin will remain in place until the next round of strips. This is necessary to prevent inadvertent fold-over of the strips during stitching. Add the second strip for patch #1 on the opposite side of the center square, pin, turn the foundation, stitch, press, and pin as before (Fig. 2-22).

With the foundation towards you, fold it back on the stitching line for patch #2 and trim any excess fabric that extends past the ¼" seam allowance for that stitching line (Fig. 2-23). It is a good idea to pull the two overrun stitches at each end of the previous sewing line away from the paper (Fig. 2-24). This will make the trimming, as well as the ultimate removal of the foundation, easier.

Cut two pieces of the dark strip the length of the seam line for patch #2 plus ½" for seam allowance. This is easiest to measure from the top or drawn side of the foundation (Fig. 2-25).

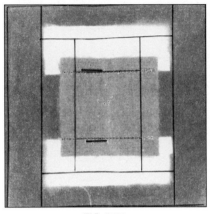

FIG. 2-21.

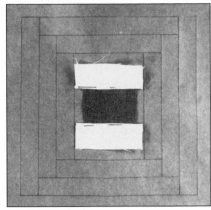

FIG. 2-22.

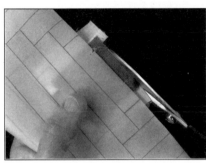

FIG. 2-23

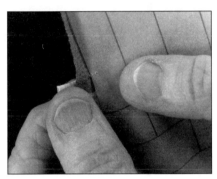

FIG. 2-24

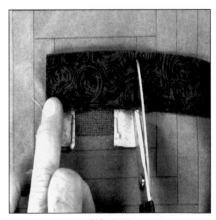

FIG. 2-25

Lay the first piece, right side down, along the seam line for patch #2, matching the cut edge to the trimmed seam allowance. Using the same technique as for patch #1, pin, stitch, press, pin, and trim as before (Fig. 2-26). Continue piecing, pressing, and trimming, using light strips for the odd numbered patches and dark strips for the even.

We suggest you extend the stitching across the seam allowances at the edge of the block to provide stability to the edge when the blocks are joined.

The final outer line on the foundation is the sewing line for attaching the blocks to each other. After the last strips are sewn, pressed, and pinned in place, turn the foundation over and stay-stitch a scant ¼" outside that final line with a long basting stitch. Trim the excess foundation and fabric just beyond the stay-stitching line (Fig. 2-27).

An option when using this technique is not to cut individual pieces for each patch, but to sew them using a long strip as in technique #1, cutting after each stitching (Fig. 2-28). This avoids pinning, but there is some risk of catching excess fabric from the long strip in the seam.

When using either option for sewing strips, it is a good idea to smooth them in place as the foundation is turned fabric-side-down in preparation for stitching, to make sure the strips are lying flat and have not folded or twisted.

•**SINGLE FOUNDATION PIECING**
The third major type of foundation piecing is single foundation piecing. Its antecedent is English template piecing which is always sewn by hand. Individual paper foundations the finished size of the patch are laid on the wrong

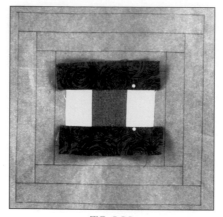

FIG. 2-26

FIG. 2-27

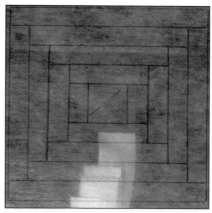

FIG. 2-28

side of the fabric with the seam allowance wrapped over the edge of the foundation and basted through all layers. The edges of each basted piece are aligned and sewn together with a small whipstitch. The foundation is ultimately removed (Fig. 2-29).

Single foundation piecing is an updated version of English piecing, avoiding the laborious basting and whipstitching, but retaining the precision of this type of piecing. Freezer or adhesive paper foundations are attached to the fabric, which is cut with the seam allowance extending ¼" beyond the foundation (Fig. 2-30). The pieces can then be joined either by hand, machine, or a combination of both. This technique can be used by itself for an entire quilt, or in combination with pressed-piecing.

Designs involving scenic patterns, animals, and flowers easily break down into units which can be worked in this manner. These types of patterns, which would involve making many one-of-a-kind templates, can be traced onto freezer paper. To avoid confusion when assembling the design, it is essential to code both the master copy and the traced copy with numbers or letters before cutting the traced copy apart (Fig. 2-31). Otherwise you will be confronted with a pile of paper pieces which won't immediately reveal their place in the larger picture.

FIG. 2-29 ANTIQUE ENGLISH PIECING

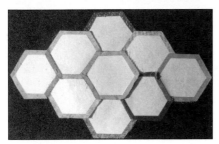

FIG. 2-30.

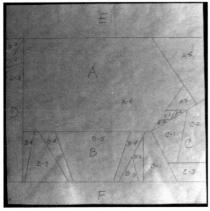

FIG. 2-31.

We occasionally sew delicate set-in areas by hand, even in a design primarily sewn by machine, in order to control multiple matching points.

HYBRID FOUNDATION TECHNIQUES

These techniques use foundations but vary from the three major foundation techniques since they are used to prepare fabrics for piecing rather than to construct blocks directly. Two techniques are variations of popular quick-piecing techniques.

•STRIP PIECING ON FREEZER PAPER

This technique is used in the same way as conventional strip piecing. Long strips are sewn together to create pieced fabric which is re-cut into patches using either a measurement or a template. These are re-sewn into a design. The process is faster and more accurate than cutting and sewing individual pieces.

Press-piecing the strips onto freezer paper, adhering each one to the paper as it is added, can control the twisting and stretching often encountered when using strip piecing. Using *under* pressed-piecing, sewing on drawn lines, guarantees each strip will be the desired width for its entire length. This ensures accuracy when the strip-set is cut and the pieces are re-sewn.

Foundation strip piecing is especially valuable when piecing either narrow strips or bias strips, both of which can be difficult to control. This method also is important when working with patterns with strong value contrast which depend on extreme precision in assembly for their impact. Accuracy is further ensured because marking a measurement or drawing around a template on freezer paper is easier than drawing on the unstabilized fabric (Fig. 2-32).

FIG. 2-32.

•FOUNDATIONS FOR SHEETED TRIANGLES

Another widely used quick-piecing technique is the process of making many identical half-square triangle units by sheeting triangles. This is done by placing two pieces of fabric right sides together and drawing a grid of squares on the wrong side of one of the fabrics. Diagonal lines are drawn through each square. By stitching ¼" on each side of each diagonal line, and then cutting the fabric apart on all horizontal, vertical, and diagonal lines, you create many pre-sewn squares of identical half-square triangles.

The size of the drawn squares is determined by adding ⅞" to the desired finished right-angle triangle. This measurement allows for all of the seam allowances, including that of the diagonal cut across the square. For instance, if you want the right-angle side of the finished triangle to measure 2", you would draw a 2⅞" grid.

The distortion often caused by drawing directly on the fabric, or not sewing a consistent ¼" seam allowance, can result in inaccu-

19

rate squares. To compensate, many quilters add a full inch rather than ⅞" to the size of the square and true up the finished pieces.

By using the *under* pressed-pieced method of sewing on the seam line with a paper foundation, it is possible to create identical half-square triangle units from a grid using the correct ⅞" measurement. This is not true pressed-piecing because the foundation is used only as a guide to sew and cut, with the pressing done after the foundation is removed.

Draw a grid with squares the size of the finished half square triangle plus ⅞". In addition, draw sewing lines ¼" on each side of all of the diagonal lines. Pin this foundation on top of the two pieces of fabric that have been placed right sides together, and stitch on the sewing lines. Cut apart on the horizontal, vertical, and diagonal cutting lines. Remove the paper from the triangles, open, and press carefully along the grainlines to prevent skewing the square (Fig. 2-33). Quarter-square triangles can be done in the same manner, adding 1¼" to the square grid and drawing diagonally through the squares in both directions (Fig. 2-34).

It also is possible to press-piece strips of half-square triangles, using either *top* or *under*

pressed-piecing (Fig 2-35). These strips could be used as sawteeth in a border, in a design such as Pine Burr (Block Plates 53, 54), or assembled into a pattern such as a Pine Tree by joining rows of the required numbers of half-square triangle units. Pre-printed papers for these strips are available in sheets and in rolls. See Resource List.

FIG. 2-33
Sheeted half-square triangles using a foundation. This configuration of diagonal lines, originally developed by Barbara Johannah, avoids sewing through the tips of adjacent triangles.

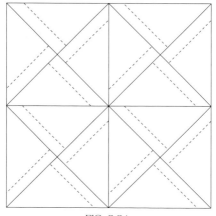

FIG. 2-34.
Grid for sheeted quarter-square triangles, also developed by Barbara Johannah.

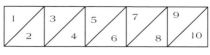

FIG. 2-35.

•FREEZER PAPER FOUNDATIONS FOR FOLDED PATTERNS

This technique uses freezer paper foundations as templates to prepare fabric for folded piecing techniques such as Prairie Points, Folded Stars, and Cathedral Window designs. The accuracy of these patterns is dependent on the precision and sharpness of the folded fabric which is used to create the units of the designs. Freezer paper provides control and precision for the size and configuration of the fabric. Foundations for prairie points are available commercially. See Resource List.

Jean Mihran, of Niskayuna, NY, fell heir to a pre-cut set of muslin squares for a Cathedral Window quilt. She ironed a 6" square of freezer paper onto a 6½" muslin square and pressed the seam allowances over the paper. The square was then folded on the pattern lines and pressed so the angles and points at each corner were sharp and fit together exactly. When the paper was removed, the fabric retained its pressed shape and each window square matched the others perfectly.

Chapter 3

FORMATS AND FINE POINTS OF
FOUNDATION PIECING

In addition to the options of foundation materials, marking methods, and piecing techniques, you also have some choices in formats for foundation work. In this chapter, we will examine the formats as well as explore the fine points of foundation piecing.

FORMATS

The formats include **whole blocks** of whatever shape; **segments** or portions of blocks; and **single foundations** of varying shapes. These can be worked in combination with each other and also with conventional piecing.

The whole block format using pressed-piecing is the most familiar. It involves whole blocks, whether squares, triangles, rectangles, or diamonds, which can be completely pieced without a break. Piecing can begin from the center (Fig. 3-1a), from a side, or from a corner (Fig. 3-1b). Typical

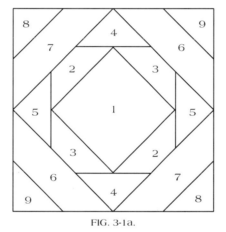

FIG. 3-1a.

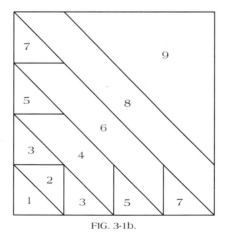

FIG. 3-1b.

traditional examples of whole block foundation piecing include string, crazy patch, and any of the Log Cabin family. Reviewing pieced pattern encyclopedias, it is possible to find many more examples of blocks that can be pieced in this way. We have included a representative number of blocks in this book that usually have not been worked on foundations. There are many more candidates for you to discover.

The single foundation format also is easily defined. As we said earlier, it is based on English piecing where each piece has a separate foundation. The single pieces are joined together to make a block, giving the quiltmaker the advantages of stability, precision, and control of the fabric not available with conventional piecing (Fig. 3-2).

Every block could be broken down entirely into single foundations. However it is time consum-

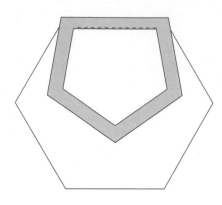

FIG. 3-2.

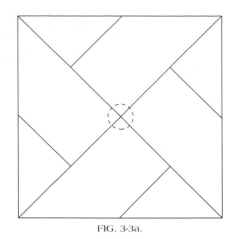

FIG. 3-3a.

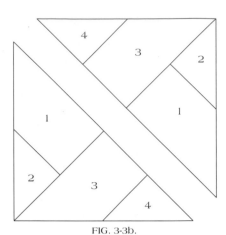

FIG. 3-3b.

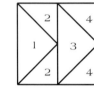

FIG. 3-4a.

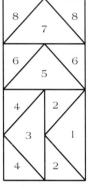

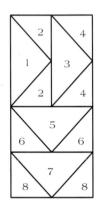

FIG. 3-4b.

ing to match and pin the individual pieces. Of all the foundation piecing techniques, pressed-piecing is the fastest, most efficient, and most precise. In order to press-piece, you should be able to sew each added piece along the entire edge of the previous piece. If there is an area where a seam crosses or abuts a line of the pattern, or a pivot or set-in piece is necessary, pressed-piecing cannot continue without dividing the block into segments (Fig. 3-3a and b).

In our last book, we took foundation piecing into a new arena by opening its use to patterns which could not be foundation pieced in a whole block because of its geometry. We introduced the concept of breaking the block into segments whenever pressed-piecing could not continue, treating each segment as an entity to be joined to another segment, whether press-pieced, single foundation, or conventional.

To understand and benefit from the concept of a segment format,

you need to learn to read a block with an eye to how it can be broken down for easy and efficient construction. The block may divide evenly into half, quarter, or eighth segments. It may divide asymmetrically, or it may be necessary to use a single foundation or conventional piecing in a given area. Realize that there may be more than one way to do this for any block.

When first examining a block, be aware it may be possible to press-piece a segment in one direction but not in the other. Dutchman's Puzzle is a good example. It is readily apparent

that the block can be broken into quarter segments (Fig. 3-4a). It can also be done as half segments (Fig. 3-4b). You must begin at the appropriate side of the rectangle in order to avoid being interrupted by a cross-seam.

A more complex example can be seen in Combination Star. A Nine-Patch pattern, it can be broken down into four press-pieced patches and four patches using the hybrid quarter-square triangle technique (Fig. 3-5). A more efficient possibility is to break the block diagonally. This gives you two different pairs of corner foundations plus one foundation in the center for a total of five segments (Fig. 3-6).

Some patterns cannot be press-pieced without changing the direction of a seam; sometimes adding or even eliminating one seam entirely is necessary (Fig. 3-7a and b).

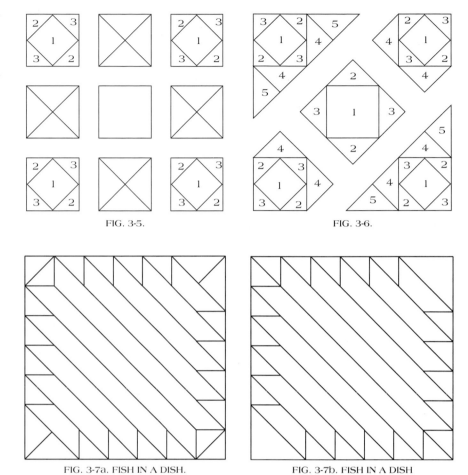

FIG. 3-5.

FIG. 3-6.

FIG. 3-7a. FISH IN A DISH.

FIG. 3-7b. FISH IN A DISH with corner lines changed.

• • • •

ESSENTIALLY WHAT YOU DO WHEN YOU DETERMINE A PATTERN CAN BE CONSTRUCTED IN SEGMENTS IS:

• Decide how to break it into components

• Create it on a foundation

• Code it for piecing order

• Cut it into segments

• Piece and reassemble the segments into a block

We have divided the patterns in the book into categories, according to these formats. Most of the whole block formats are pieced beginning in the center although two are pieced across the block from the corner. One is a pair of triangular blocks.

The segmented blocks that are entirely press-pieced are divided into half, quarter, eighth, and asymmetrical divisions. Some of

the half blocks are divided vertically and some diagonally. One, The Palm, we show as a block divided into diagonal halves. Some versions of this pattern show four Palms as one block, which would make our division an eighth of the total.

Some quarter blocks are squares, others are triangular segments. All of them, and most of the eighth blocks, have identical segments. Two of the latter involve two different segments. All of the asymmetrically divided blocks have two or more segment shapes.

We have included several blocks made entirely with single foundation piecing, and a number of blocks that involve combinations of single and pressed-piecing formats. Some single patches have curves. These may be more easily done with conventional piecing, especially when being joined to a press-pieced curved segment.

Two blocks use half-square triangle foundation piecing. There are another two blocks for which we recommend using strip piecing on a freezer paper foundation, although they could also be pieced directly on foundation segments.

Study all the blocks, not only to choose which ones you would like to piece, but also to practice your skills in reading a block and breaking it down into possible segments.

CUTTING FABRIC

In the Courthouse Steps block we used to introduce you to *top* and *under* pressed-piecing, cutting fabric for the center and strips with the ¼" seam allowance included was straightforward. When *top* pressed-piecing any block except crazy patch and string designs, exact measurements are always used.

With *under* pressed-piecing, exact measurements are not as essential. The only requirement for a piece of fabric is that it be large enough to cover the area of the block it is designed for, with adequate seam allowance on all sides. With many blocks, cutting each piece to the exact measurement plus ¼" seam allowance is neither necessary nor desirable because of the *under* pressed-piecing construction process.

There are several ways to cut fabric for *under* pressed-pieced blocks. It is simple to cut the first piece of fabric placed on the block to the exact size, since it can be centered on the patch. This provides an edge with the proper seam allowance against which to place the fabric for the second patch without trimming.

In theory, each piece could be added this way; in practice, it is easy to misalign fabric so it does not cover the patch when open and pressed. For this reason, we pre-cut the fabric shapes so the seam allowance is ½", trimming the fabric to size after it is sewn in place. This works well for strips, rectangles, and squares. Since they are pressed up to the next sewing line, they will cover the area of the next strip without any problem.

Triangles are another matter. It is easy to cut a triangle too small and not have it cover the area after it is sewn. It is possible to cover any space with a large chunk of fabric, to be certain to have enough to cover the patch. However this method pays no attention to grainline and the resulting patch may have a skewed look to it, especially if any of the fabrics are printed directionally. The advantages of quick cutting and foundation piecing do not eliminate the need for grainline control.

As a general rule, the outside edge of the block should be on grain or aligned with a fabric print. Diamonds and triangles used as star points are best cut with the grain running down the middle through the point, both in order to enhance the visual effect and to have consistent bias edges.

We unequivocally recommend

the use of rough-cut templates. The term "rough-cut" describes how we cut for *under* pressed-piecing that gives the basic shape of the piece, retains the proper grain of the fabric, and adds a larger-than-usual seam allowance. It allows for the fact that angles can be deceptive when sewn and turned over. Rough cutting both saves cutting time and gives a fudge factor when piecing. The ease of piecing more than compensates for the small amount of extra fabric used. It definitely saves time correcting misaligned pieces.

Fabric for right-angle half-square triangles can be rough cut using a variation of quick-cutting techniques. Instead of adding ⅞" to the measurement of the side of the right triangle, add at least 1½" to give you a larger seam allowance and a little more placement room (Fig. 3-8). When cutting four triangles from a square, with each hypotenuse on-grain, instead of adding 1¼" to the measurement of the hypotenuse, add 2" (Fig. 3-9).

Asymmetric shapes and triangles with angles other than 45° are more difficult to cut to both retain the grainline and sew in place so they fully cover the patch when opened. To cut these shapes easily and correctly, make an extra copy of the full-size pattern, marking the proper grainline on each different piece. The fabric

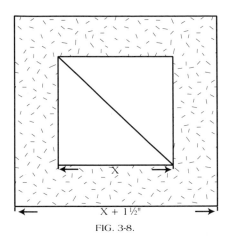

FIG. 3-8.

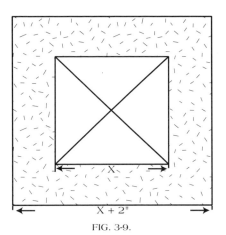

FIG. 3-9.

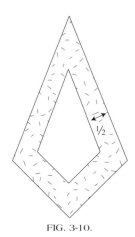

FIG. 3-10.

pieces will be cut out by laying or pinning the pattern pieces on the fabric and rough cutting them with ½" seam allowance on all sides (Fig. 3-10). The exact angle of a point is crucial for placement and final fit of the patch in pressed-piecing. The skinnier the angle, the more important it is to cut the shape of that angle accurately.

When you use *under* pressed-piecing, you sew on the reverse of the drawn pattern, with the fabric on the underside of the foundation. Therefore, the rough-cut templates must be placed not only on the correct grain, but also on the wrong side of the fabric to cut the patches. This is essential for asymmetric shapes and triangles; otherwise the angles will be reversed.

Some patterns have identical segments, often rotated in placement. If you wish to cut more than one piece at a time, you must have all the fabric layered so all the wrong sides face up.

This will give you pieces that are identical and identically oriented. Other patterns have segments that are direct mirror images. The fabric for cutting these must have right or wrong sides together, to produce two patches with mirror images to match the design.

If you wish to cut fabric to position a specific motif, you can cut an exact template with a ¼" seam allowance and position it carefully on the foundation. You may want to use *top* pressed-piecing for this fabric to have the fabric visible as it is sewn in place. This can be done even if you are using *under* pressed-piecing for the rest of the block. Or this can be done in reverse; for instance, the blocks for SOHO SUNDAY (Gallery Plate 35) were mainly pieced with *top* pressed-piecing in crazy quilt style without marking the foundation. But when specific shapes were desired, Dixie drew them on the back of the foundation and used *under* pressed-piecing while sewing the shapes.

FIG. 3-11.

As you did in the *under* pressed-pieced sample block in Chapter Two, each time a patch is open and pressed, fold back the foundation on the next sewing line and trim the seam allowance of the piece just sewn to ¼" past the next sewing line for an accurate placement line for the next patch.

On a short edge, we eyeball the seam; on a longer edge, you can use a ruler and rotary cutter (Fig. 3-11). Don't get distracted and cut along the fold line; you'll have no seam allowance! If you fail to trim the seam and line up the next patch along the edge of the previous one, the seam allowance will be so large that even a rough-cut patch may not cover the space it needs to when opened up (Fig. 3-12).

FIG. 3-12.

Even with pre-trimming, we sometimes retrim a seam allowance after sewing to a scant ¼" or less. This eliminates bulk in small pieces and points, and avoids shadow through when you are dealing with light and dark fabrics.

MIRROR IMAGE

When you work with *under* pressed-piecing or with single foundation piecing using freezer paper, remember you are sewing a design in a mirror image from the one you have drawn on the top side of the foundation. Placing the fabric on the undrawn side of the foundation, with the wrong side of the fabric against the foundation, will make the finished design reversed from the drawing. If the design is symmetrical, it will look the same. If the design or any element of it is asymmetrical, the completed block will be oriented in the opposite direction from the pattern.

In other words, Starry Path (Block Plates 22, 23) twirling to the right in the drawing will twirl to the left in the fabric block. Sheep Safely Grazing (Block Plate 52) facing right in the drawing, will face left in fabric. This will not matter unless esthetic considerations or the design of your quilt plays a part in your preference for block layout.

If you wish to counter a mirror image and have the blocks look exactly like the pattern, there are several ways to do so. The easiest is to use a transparent foundation, such as tracing paper or lightweight tear-away interfacing. The lines of the pattern will be visible from both sides, and it is a simple matter to mark "fabric" on the drawn side of the pattern, and to stitch on the lines that show through the back.

Remember, if you have needle punched foundations on paper, the top side will be smooth and the underside slightly rough. We usually place the fabric on the rough side. If mirror imaging is not a problem, the rough side is the more desirable side on which to lay the fabric because it helps keep the fabric from shifting. To prevent a mirror image, lay the fabric on the smooth side of the foundation and stitch with the rough side up.

To reverse a mirror image when using nontransparent foundations such as freezer paper or fabric,

you have to reverse the master pattern. This can be done by putting it on a light table or up to a window and redrawing the lines on the wrong side of the pattern. You can accomplish the same thing by placing a sheet of dressmaker's carbon paper, carbon side up, under the pattern and drawing over the lines. Then use the re-marked side to trace the pattern.

Some patterns, such as The Palm (Block Plate 15), have a mirror image inherent in the design, which can cause a potential problem. The pattern is based on a right and a left side along the diagonal line. This is of no concern if you are consistent about the side of the foundation on which you piece. We write "up" or "fabric" directly on each foundation segment of a pattern before cutting them apart.

Be sure you always piece on the same side of all foundation segments in a pattern regardless of the design, or you may create a mirror image where none existed. Then it will be impossible to piece the pattern as designed, and you will have to re-do the segment.

PIECING DETAILS

Under pressed-piecing is one of the most precise ways to piece. However, no block is immune to careless workmanship. A wrinkled foundation, hasty tracing, and inattentive sewing all can negate the advantages.

The basic process of pressed-piecing assumes that the added piece of fabric, when opened out after stitching, will cover the patch it is designed to cover with ample seam allowance and correct grainline placement. Even with rough-cut templates and a properly trimmed seam allowance on the previously sewn patch, it is possible to misposition the new patch. The wrong edge can be laid down, and/or the patch can be off-center causing an end not to cover (Fig. 3-13). This is particularly true when *under* press-piecing angled pieces.

The simplest way to avoid this problem is to lay the patch in place, right side up, on the right side of the block in its proper position. Center the patch, making sure there is ½" seam allowance at each end and that it will cover its space. Then flip the patch over on the edge to which it will be sewn, retaining the position (Fig. 3-14). Even when the patch is properly laid in place and you have aligned it for sewing, it may look wrong. Eyeballing, which normally stands us in good stead, will not necessarily work here. We frequently pin the patch in place along the sewing line, and open it out to check that it is correctly positioned.

Working on a foundation does not preclude production piecing techniques such as chain piecing. It is often as efficient to chain piece,

FIG. 3-13.

FIG. 3-14.

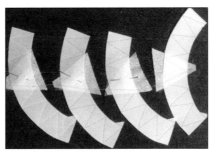

FIG. 3-15.

press, trim, and restitch with foundations as with conventional piecing (Fig. 3-15). On a block with complex piecing or coloration, doing the same step at the same time on all the blocks helps avoid errors. In such cases, we complete one block that is used as a guide for the others.

On many blocks more than one piece can be added before trimming. This is especially true of center-based blocks. For example, in the Courthouse Steps block, we can piece both opposite sides in a row before pressing and trimming. The pieces can be sewn in place, pressed, and trimmed at the same time.

Points can be a particular problem. They must be drawn and sewn exactly; the tip of a point has to be just a hair inside a subsequent crossing line to avoid the point being oversewn. As you approach a tip on either line of stitching, stitch on the inner side of the lines. However, your traced line may be slightly inaccurate, or a previously stitched line may have been sewn slightly off-line. When stitching along a line which forms the second side of an angle, aim the sewing machine needle so you are directly on the line or directly in the middle of the angle if the line has shifted. Using foundations and *under* pressed-piecing, you have the unique opportunity to correct small deviations and make perfect points.

With pressed-piecing techniques, you don't always have control of the direction the seams will lie. This may have an effect on the look of the block and the look of quilting. Sometimes you may have more than one option for the direction in which to piece, which will give you some choice.

For instance, you may be able to start in the center and sew out on either side, or start at one edge and proceed across the foundation (Fig. 3-16).

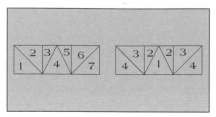

FIG. 3-16.

Some quiltmakers opt to use single foundation piecing for parts of patterns which could be press-pieced in order to control the seam directions for final pressing and quilting.. For instance, if you wish to quilt in the ditch in the background on either side of sharp points such as in the Mariner's Compass, you may not want to press-piece the segments containing those points since the seam allowances would be pressed out against the background fabric.

Another aspect of piecing direction is the potential of a dark fabric to shadow through a lighter fabric laid on top. When starting a block, if you have a choice of which piece to put down first, always put a dark fabric on top of a light one. When it is necessary to put a lighter fabric on top, grade the darker seam or extend the lighter one with a slightly wider seam allowance. Once the piecing has proceeded past a shadow through, it is more difficult to correct than when it

occurs with conventional piecing.

As with any sewing, mistakes happen and you need to take out stitches. Obviously, it is easier to un-sew on a permanent foundation than on a temporary one, but ripping out stitches even from a thin paper foundation can be done without mishap. The trick is to always rip between fabric and fabric rather than between fabric and paper. Should you tear the foundation, it can be taped together or patched by pressing freezer paper across the tear.

After stitching a line, if there is any doubt whether your points are sharp or if the patch will cover the drawn area adequately, open it out and check before pressing. Ripping out stitches is much easier when they have just been sewn in, before stitch setting and pressing.

JOINING SEGMENTS AND BLOCKS

Your initial foundation choice is made with several considerations, such as the marking technique, the piecing technique, the type of pattern, and perhaps, the ease of foundation removal.

Your choice of how the foundation is prepared is also a factor in joining the blocks and segments. One advantage of making the foundation the size of the finished block without the seam allowances included is that the

cut edge of the foundation becomes a stitching guide for joining the blocks (Fig. 3-17). Another advantage is that removal of the foundation is easier when it is not stitched into the seam allowance. Freezer paper foundations hold the fabric at the edges of the block firmly even though the paper does not extend into the seam allowance. Any other foundation material that does not include the seam allowance must have the fabric securely pinned or basted at long edges and corners. This keeps the fabric taut and prevents it from folding or twisting. It also prevents the foundation from slipping and distorting the sewing line.

FIG. 3-17.

A foundation cut to include the seam allowance and basted at the edge to hold the fabric has a secure guide line for joining blocks (Fig. 3-18), but removing the basting stitches and the foundation from the seam allowance is more time consuming.

When using sharp value contrast fabrics in pressed-piecing, thread

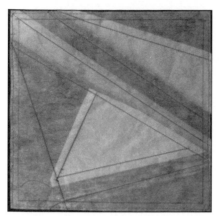

FIG. 3-18.

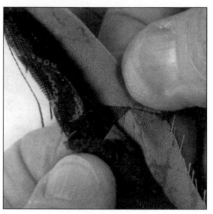

FIG. 3-21.

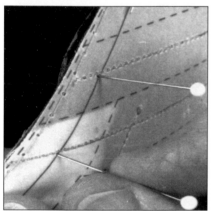

FIG. 3-19.

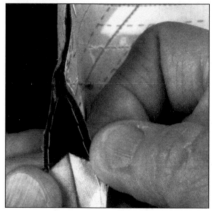

FIG. 3-22.

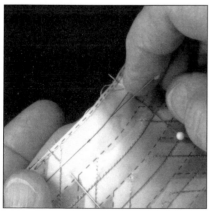

FIG. 3-20.

color is important. It is crucial when joining segments, whether press pieced or single, and blocks. It usually is not necessary to change both top and bottom thread in the sewing machine; a neutral color in the bobbin with a dark matching color on top helps make the stitches unobtrusive.

When stitching two segments or blocks together, it is helpful to have the side with the most points upmost so you can sew directly on those points. We stab pins at each point or cross seam of the top segment, matching to the points and cross seams of the under segment (Fig. 3-19). Pin along the lines (Fig. 3-20). Place the right sides of two segments together, pinning together the beginning and ending points of the sewing line. It is essential to begin and end exactly at the point of each sewing line. If your stitching has varied even slightly, pin the point right next to the last stitch of the cross seam so your fabric joint appears straight and accurate.

For tricky joins, with many lines coming into one point forming angles, bend back the two segments at the seam lines so the match points are visible from the right side. Position the match points together exactly (Fig. 3-21). Where lines extend into the seam allowance at an angle, they will form a chevron when properly matched (Fig. 3-22). Pinch the seg-

ments together firmly and pin vertically, using two pins if necessary.

Since the fabric may have moved slightly on the segment with sewing or pressing earlier seams, you may not be able to rely solely on stabbing pins through the drawn points. As a final step before stitching the two segments together, open them out and check not only that the points and angles are stabilized correctly, but that the outer seam lines of the block will be continuous. It is easy to move a segment up or down a small amount and lose the smooth outer line of the block (Fig. 3-23a and b).

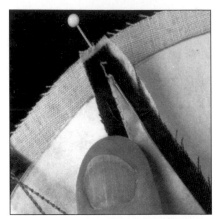

FIG. 3-23a.

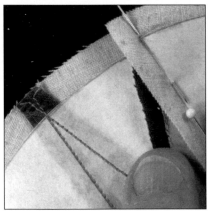

FIG. 3-23b.

Stitching on the inside edge of the seam line when joining segments or blocks seems to give better points. A presser foot with a line down the center is helpful for stitching directly on the sewing line. Some open-toe presser feet do not hold the fabric securely.

When joining segments, be aware that foundations resting against the feed dogs are not held as firmly as fabric would be. You will need to control the piece so it does not slip. Freezer paper is especially prone to this.

Some segments need to be joined at an angle with a two-step set-in process. Setting in is most easily done with single foundations onto single foundations, or single foundations onto press-pieced segments. Two press-pieced segments can be set-in only if the angle is shallow, such as in the Sunflower (Block Plates 71, 72). Right angles are best set-in using separate single foundation segments.

It is essential to stitch the two fabric sections together along the seamline without catching any seam allowances at the set-in point. Pin the points, and pin along the stitching line to anchor the seam (Fig. 3-24). To have easy access to the sewing line, it may be necessary to bend or crease previously sewn parts of the piece out of the way. By starting at the inner point of a set-in,

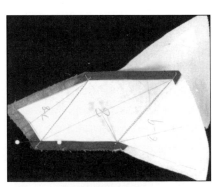

FIG. 3-24.

placing the sewing machine needle at the exact thread of the point, and stitching to the outside, you have complete control of the angle. Stitch from point to point, backstitching at both the beginning and the end of the line.

CURVES

Patterns with curved patches and segments also can be pieced using foundations. With fabric or removable interfacing foundations, it is possible to press-piece a pattern with shallow curves using either *top* or *under* pressed-piecing. June Ryker uses bias-cut strips and *top* pressed-piecing to construct curved Log Cabin designs.

Freezer paper can be used as a single foundation for curved segments, but joining two segments is more difficult than with conventional piecing if the curve is anything but shallow. When piecing curves, one side must be slightly stretched to fit the other and freezer paper segments are not flexible enough to be manipulated easily under the presser foot. Hand piecing may be an option for these patterns, to retain the advantages of foundation piecing and to cope with sewing curves as in Field of Daisies (Block Plate 49). If machine piecing is your choice, try Dory Sandon's method of tearing the foundation slightly at intervals to make setting in the curved piece less difficult.

A curved piece can be sewn to a curved foundation segment most easily by using conventional piecing for one segment, with the edge of the foundation pieced segment serving as a stitching guide for assembly. It is important to have an accurate sewing line on any piece without a foundation even with an exactly cut ¼" seam allowance. This can be done either by making a plastic template or by cutting one of freezer paper, which will be removed after drawing around it. Care must be taken not to distort the block by stretching the unstabilized pieces either when drawing the sewing line or when stitching the two pieces together.

When joining curves, Caryl Bryer Fallert marks the sewing line on the wrong side of the fabric of both pieces, and removes the foundations before stitching the seam. Joen Wolfrom sews a line of staystitching at the edge of the freezer paper before removing the foundations. Mia Rozmyn, in her book, credits Joen with introducing her to this technique. It not only marks the seam line, but also stabilizes the fabric as the curve is handled and sewn.

To retain fine matches and reduce bulk, we frequently press open the seams. This makes removal of temporary foundations easier, especially if the foundations do not extend into the seam allowances. Leave temporary foundations in place until blocks are joined. On a large quilt, this can be somewhat unwieldy because of the added weight. When this is the case, foundations on the interior of the quilt can be removed after the surrounding blocks are attached. However, it is a good idea to leave the complete foundations on the blocks in the outer row. This aids in accurate border measurements and avoids stretching the quilt top as the borders are added.

Temporary foundations should be removed with care to avoid tearing the stitches or stretching the fabric. You can score or crease the foundation along the stitching lines with a blunt tool such as a knitting needle, crochet hook, or a bodkin.

Chapter 4

THE PATTERNS

Quilt blocks are like garden seeds; it's what grows from them that is exciting.

We chose the blocks for this book with several goals in mind. First, of course, to show the versatility of foundation techniques for a variety of largely traditional blocks not usually pieced on foundations. Second, because we like them and believe they have the potential to make wonderful quilts and other projects. Third, because we listened to foundation enthusiasts across the country who wanted larger blocks.

Use the blocks, not only to piece, but also to study how and why they are suitable for foundation piecing. We have by no means exhausted the possibilities for blocks that can be pieced on foundations; there are many others.

With the exception of a 3" and 4" Mariner's Compass, the patterns range from 6" to 16", with the majority being 8". Most of the 6" patterns are whole blocks. Many of the ones we selected traditionally combine into four-block units

. . . .

WHEN EXAMINING ANY BLOCK, ASK YOURSELF:

•Are there advantages to piecing this block on a foundation such as stability, precision, speed, or design assistance?

•Which format is needed: whole block, segment, or single?

•What is the most efficient way to divide the block into segments, if necessary?

•Which piecing technique is best – pressed-piecing, single, or a combination of either or both with conventional piecing?

•Which press-piecing method is suitable – *top* pressed-piecing, or *under* pressed-piecing?

•What is the piecing order of press-pieced blocks or segments?

to achieve their graphic potential, thereby forming a 12" block. The 8" blocks are all segmented. They can be used alone, although many of them combine to make 16" blocks. Two blocks are 16".

We chose these sizes to fit within the feasible parameters of book form. The sizes are not only practical for publication, but are also versatile for bed quilts, wall quilts, and myriad other projects that creative quilters devise. To assist those who want either larger or smaller blocks, each pattern is categorized for drafting purposes. It is a simple matter to reduce or enlarge most of these blocks; we list books in the Bibliography to assist you.

In the color section for the blocks, we show some patterns twice, to demonstrate the different graphics achieved through coloration. Our sources, unless otherwise noted, are *The Encyclopedia of Pieced Patterns* by Barbara Brackman, and three volumes of *Key to 1000 Quilt Patterns* by Judy Rehmel.

The pattern page for each block includes a small diagram of the block showing the segment division, if any. A legend includes the color plate for the pattern, the size, the segments, if any, the piecing technique(s) used, and the drafting category. Pertinent piecing information and directions are included on the page.

Where applicable, we have included small drawings of related or derivative patterns. They are either similar in design, piecing division, or both. They may not have the same drafting category or segment divisions. For instance, we include Kaleidoscope as a related pattern to Key West Beauty. Although drafted in the same way, the more elaborate Key West Beauty must be pieced in four segments rather than the two required for Kaleidoscope.

The whole block patterns arc printed as such. The segmented blocks show one of each segment printed in its entirety where possible, and identified by a letter. Some segments have fold lines indicated, which means they need to be doubled at the fold line when traced.

All the pattern lines are sewing lines and are applicable to *under* pressed-piecing and single foundation piecing. The patterns can be converted to *top* pressed-piecing with the addition of fabric placement lines ¼" outside the sewing lines. See Fig. 2-17.

The piecing order for each block or segment is printed on all patterns. As we did with the Courthouse Steps block in Chapter 2, we have given patches the same number when it doesn't matter which one is sewn first. Note that many patterns can be press-pieced in one direction only.

We indicate when rough-cut templates are advisable, or when fabric can most easily be cut

• • • •

FOR CLARITY AND CONSISTENCY IN LAY OUT

*All the press-pieced blocks are shown with separate segments. If you wish to draw the entire block, you will need to fit the segments together within the block outline.

*A section of the single segment block patterns is drawn so each different segment is shown in its proper place. To draw the entire block, you will need to extrapolate from this pattern.

*The combination blocks are drawn with the press-pieced segments attached to their respective single segments so it is easy to draw the entire block. The segment divisions are shown both on the block diagram and on the pattern.

using quick-cutting techniques for strips or triangles. To keep the grainline of right-angle triangles consistent throughout a block, we use half-square triangles and quarter-square triangles depending on the orientation of the patches. All fabric, however cut, must have generous seam allowances added.

Because we generally choose temporary foundations of tracing paper, lightweight removable interfacing, or freezer paper, we have written the directions assuming a sewing machine will be used. Any of these patterns can be adapted for hand sewing, but this is almost impossible to do when using paper foundations. We have noted several instances, when using single foundations, where hand sewing is preferable.

After you have chosen the block, select the foundation material and the marking method you wish to use. We have indicated our choice of material where appropriate.

Trace the pattern onto the foundation. To replicate the drawn pattern exactly, you should move the ruler slightly off the printed lines of the pattern to allow for the depth of the pencil line. To ensure accuracy at points and crossings, make a pencil dot and position your ruler so the drawn line goes through that dot exactly. When tracing a pattern, it is most efficient to draw all the lines in one direction at one time.

You have two options when tracing the segmented blocks. The first is to draw the entire block, rotating or reversing segments as needed. The second is to trace each segment separately on a foundation. The first method offers more certain accuracy as the block is reassembled, since the segments were fitted into and cut from the same foundation drawn as a whole block. With multiple identical segments, the second method is faster and more efficient but can be confusing when mirror image segments are involved.

When drawing the entire block, we suggest you begin with a square the size of the finished block. Divide the square into the segments indicated, and trace those segments from the pattern. The advantage of doing this rather than tracing the segments on individual foundations is that all lines of the pattern will match perfectly. Unless you are only making one block, make a master pattern and use it to mark all the foundations in your project rather than going through this process with each block.

Cut the foundation apart on the segment lines, leaving a seam allowance on the outside of the block on all sides if you desire. This method does not give you a seam allowance on the interior seams of the segment; you must be careful to trim excess fabric ¼" beyond those sides of the segment. As previously explained, the cut edge of the foundation will serve as the stitching guide on those seams.

If you choose the second option of tracing each segment separately, you can add the seam allowance on all sides. In this case, the edges of all the segments can be secured with basting before joining them.

If you use transparent foundations with either tracing method, be aware that a transparent foundation lends itself to confusion more easily. Mark "top" on each segment so you do not inadvertently reverse it when piecing. If you have drawn the whole block, mark the segments before cutting them out. If you draw the segments separately, take care not to reverse them when marking them. Note your color choices and piecing order on the segments if necessary.

BLOCK PLATES

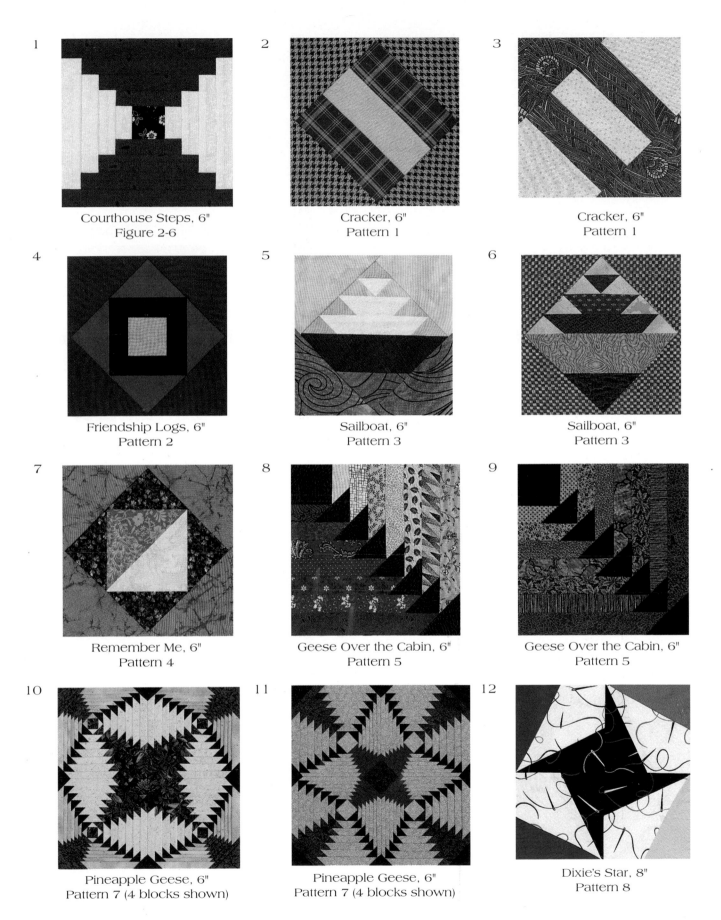

1 — Courthouse Steps, 6"
Figure 2-6

2 — Cracker, 6"
Pattern 1

3 — Cracker, 6"
Pattern 1

4 — Friendship Logs, 6"
Pattern 2

5 — Sailboat, 6"
Pattern 3

6 — Sailboat, 6"
Pattern 3

7 — Remember Me, 6"
Pattern 4

8 — Geese Over the Cabin, 6"
Pattern 5

9 — Geese Over the Cabin, 6"
Pattern 5

10 — Pineapple Geese, 6"
Pattern 7 (4 blocks shown)

11 — Pineapple Geese, 6"
Pattern 7 (4 blocks shown)

12 — Dixie's Star, 8"
Pattern 8

BLOCK PLATES

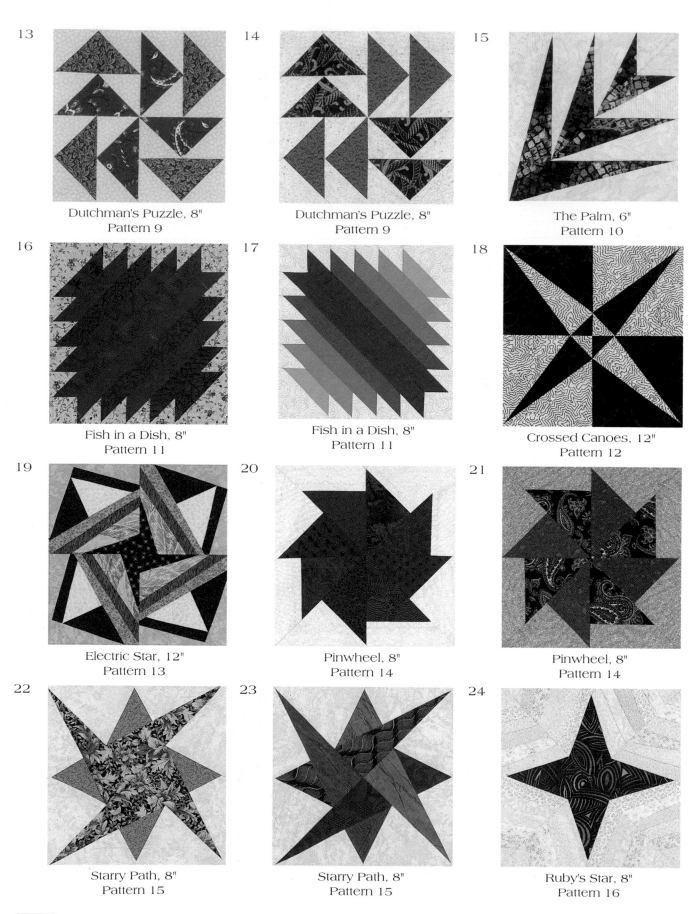

13

Dutchman's Puzzle, 8"
Pattern 9

14

Dutchman's Puzzle, 8"
Pattern 9

15

The Palm, 6"
Pattern 10

16

Fish in a Dish, 8"
Pattern 11

17

Fish in a Dish, 8"
Pattern 11

18

Crossed Canoes, 12"
Pattern 12

19

Electric Star, 12"
Pattern 13

20

Pinwheel, 8"
Pattern 14

21

Pinwheel, 8"
Pattern 14

22

Starry Path, 8"
Pattern 15

23

Starry Path, 8"
Pattern 15

24

Ruby's Star, 8"
Pattern 16

BLOCK PLATES

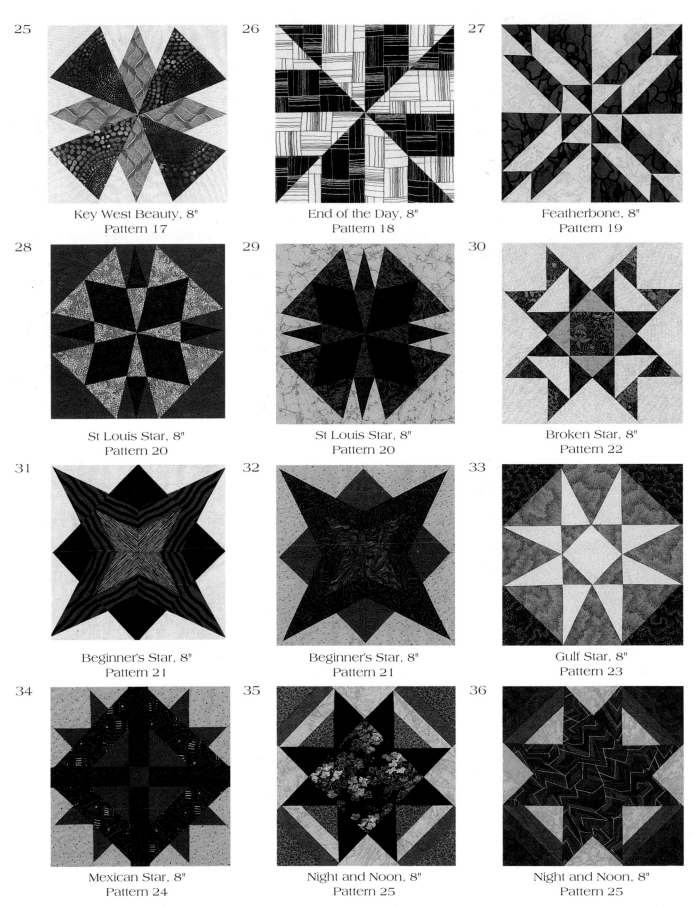

25

Key West Beauty, 8"
Pattern 17

26

End of the Day, 8"
Pattern 18

27

Featherbone, 8"
Pattern 19

28

St Louis Star, 8"
Pattern 20

29

St Louis Star, 8"
Pattern 20

30

Broken Star, 8"
Pattern 22

31

Beginner's Star, 8"
Pattern 21

32

Beginner's Star, 8"
Pattern 21

33

Gulf Star, 8"
Pattern 23

34

Mexican Star, 8"
Pattern 24

35

Night and Noon, 8"
Pattern 25

36

Night and Noon, 8"
Pattern 25

BLOCK PLATES

37

Gentleman's Fancy, 8"
Pattern 26

38

Jack in the Pulpit, 8"
Pattern 27

39

Card Trick, 8"
Pattern 28

40

Friendship Weave, 8"
Pattern 29

41

Tall Pine Tree, 8"
Pattern 30

42

Wild Goose Chase, 8"
Pattern 31

43

Butterfly, 8"
Pattern 32

44

Butterfly, 8"
Pattern 32

45

Eight•Pointed Star, 8"
Pattern 33

46

Mosaic, 8"
Pattern 34

47

Mosaic, 8"
Pattern 34

48

Interlocked Squares, 8"
Pattern 35

BLOCK PLATES

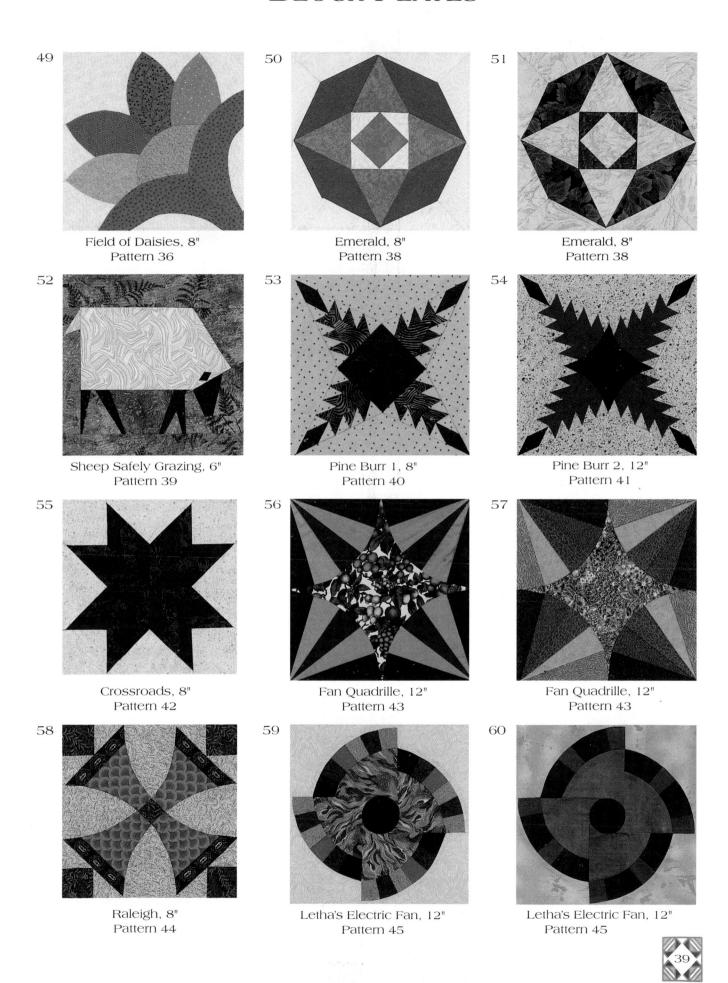

49 Field of Daisies, 8"
Pattern 36

50 Emerald, 8"
Pattern 38

51 Emerald, 8"
Pattern 38

52 Sheep Safely Grazing, 6"
Pattern 39

53 Pine Burr 1, 8"
Pattern 40

54 Pine Burr 2, 12"
Pattern 41

55 Crossroads, 8"
Pattern 42

56 Fan Quadrille, 12"
Pattern 43

57 Fan Quadrille, 12"
Pattern 43

58 Raleigh, 8"
Pattern 44

59 Letha's Electric Fan, 12"
Pattern 45

60 Letha's Electric Fan, 12"
Pattern 45

BLOCK PLATES

61

Mariner's Compass I, 8"
Pattern 46

62

Mariner's Compass II, 4"
Pattern 47

Mariner's Compass III, 3"
Pattern 48

63

Wagon Wheels, 16"
Pattern 49

64
Grandpa's Pride, 6"
Pattern 6

65

Flat Iron, 6"
Pattern 37 (3 units shown)

66

Sunflower, 16"
Pattern 50

67

Sunflower, 16"
Pattern 50

68
Golden Gates, 8"
Pattern 51

69
Golden Gates, 8"
Pattern 51

70
Basket, 8"
Pattern 52

PATTERNS
Whole Blocks

1

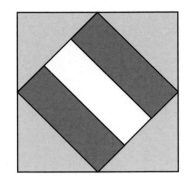

CRACKER

Block Plates 2, 3

Size: 6"
Segments: Whole block
Piecing technique: *Under* pressed-piecing
Drafting category: Four-Patch with Nine-
   Patch center

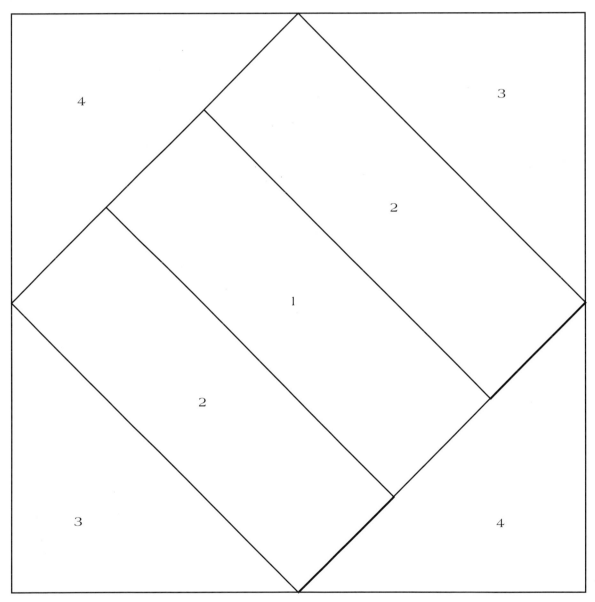

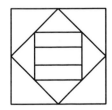

Double Anchor

Autograph

This block is a good choice to hold two signatures on the outside strips or a single signature in the middle. Use quick-cutting techniques to cut strips and half-square triangles.

PATTERNS
Whole Blocks

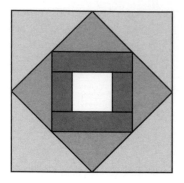

2

FRIENDSHIP LOGS

Block Plate 4, Gallery Plate 1

Size: 6"
Segments: Whole block
Piecing technique: *Under* pressed-piecing
Drafting category: Four-Patch

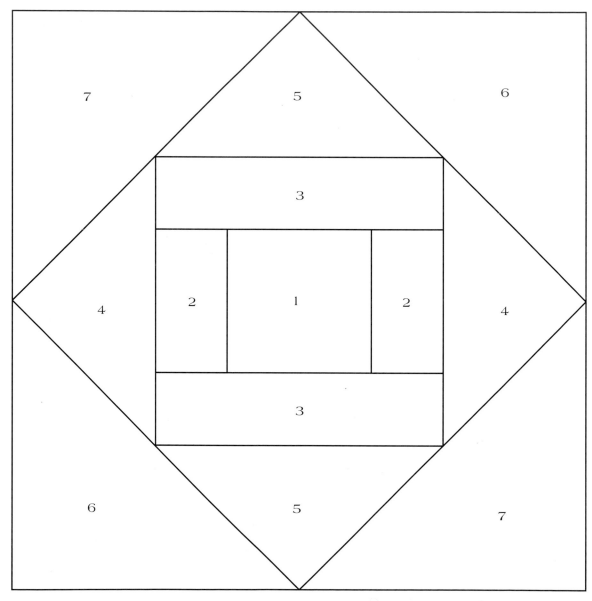

This block can be set square or on-point. If you are using this as a friendship block, decide on the set before the blocks are signed. Use quick-cutting techniques to cut strips and half-square triangles.

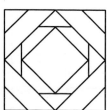

Cups & Saucers

SAILBOAT

Block Plates 5, 6

Size: 6"
Segments: Whole block
Piecing technique: *Under* pressed-piecing
Drafting category: Four-Patch

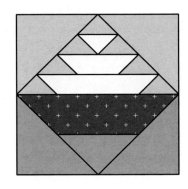

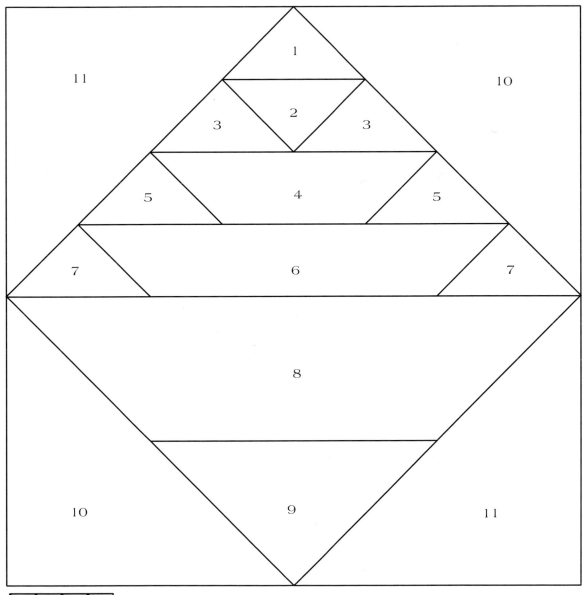

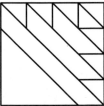

Sailboat

Note that this block can be press-pieced in only one direction. Use quick-cutting techniques to cut strips and half-square triangles.

PATTERNS
Whole Blocks

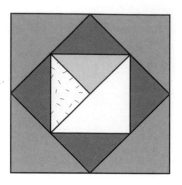

4

REMEMBER ME
Block Plate 7, Gallery Plate 2

Size: 6"
Segments: Whole block
Piecing technique: *Under* pressed-piecing
Drafting category: Four-Patch

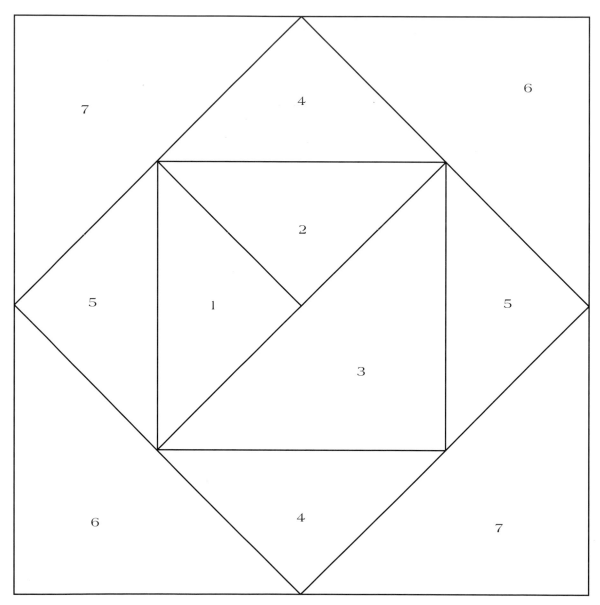

The large center triangle is an ideal place for a signature if this block is set on-point. When the signature triangle is light-colored fabric, it will be necessary to trim the seam allowances carefully to eliminate any shadow through from the previously pieced triangles. Use quick-cutting techniques to cut half-square triangles.

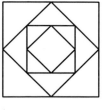

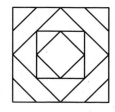

24 Triangles   Mosaic

5

GEESE OVER THE CABIN

Block Plates 8, 9

Size: 6"
Segments: Whole block
Piecing technique: *Under* pressed-piecing
Drafting category: Nine-Patch (36 grid)

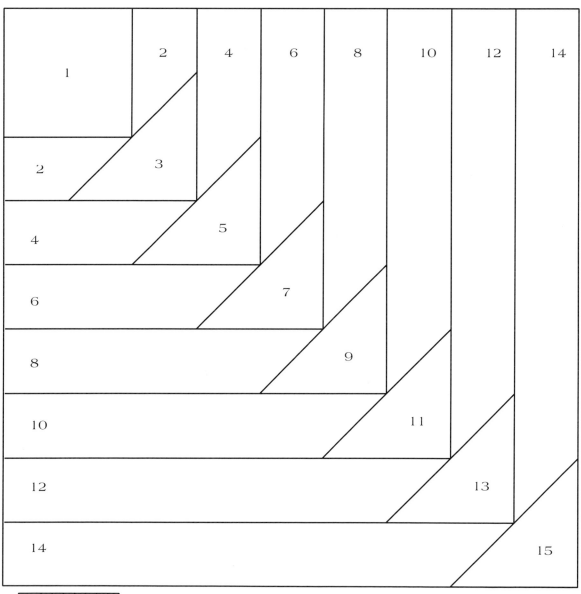

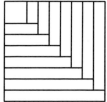

Off-Center Log Cabin

This is a Log Cabin variation with many graphic possibilities. Use quick-cutting techniques to cut strips for the logs and squares cut diagonally for the triangles.

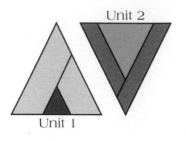

Unit 2

Unit 1

6

GRANDPA'S PRIDE

Block Plate 64, Gallery Plate 9, Figs 5-1, 5-2

Size: 6" base
Segments: Whole block
Piecing technique: *Under* pressed-piecing
Drafting category: Triangle

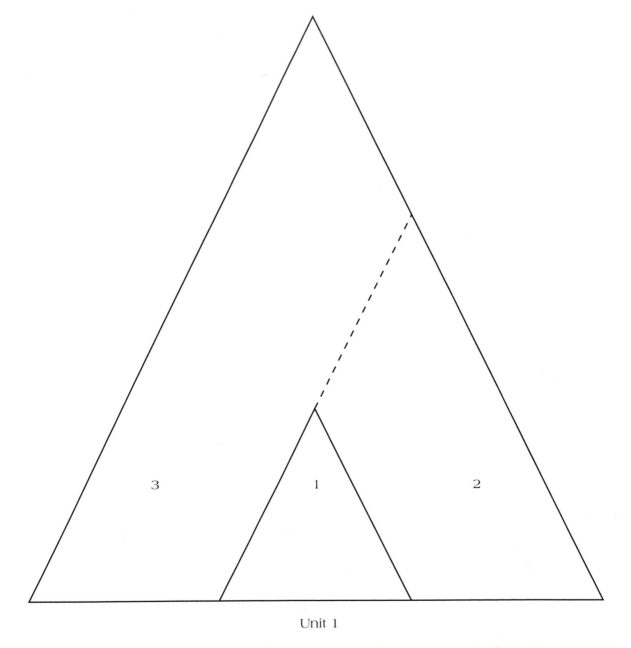

3   1   2

Unit 1

This two-unit pattern has versatility for coloration and set beyond its apparent simplicity. Freezer paper is useful to hold the side pieces in place for precise sewing. Cut strips for the sides, trimming to size after sewing.

GRANDPA'S PRIDE

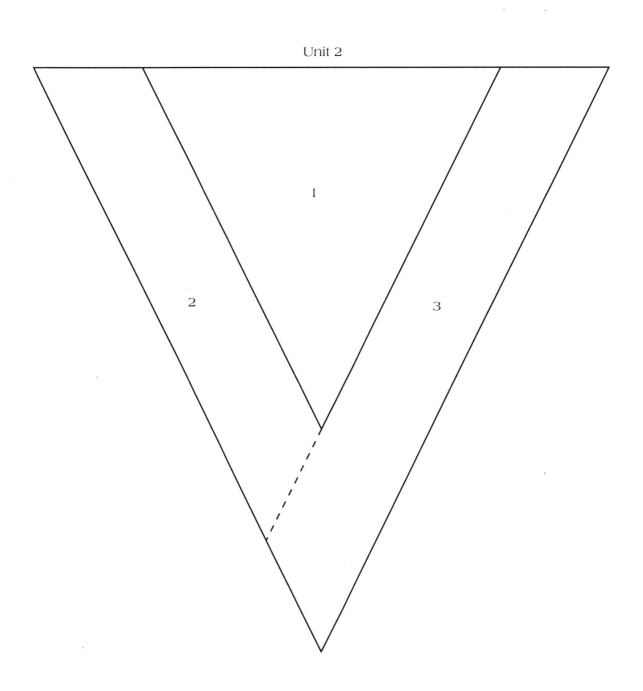

Unit 2

1

2

3

7

PINEAPPLE GEESE

Block Plates 10, 11

Size: 6"
Segments: Whole block
Piecing technique: *Under* pressed-piecing
Drafting category: Center-based

This is a Pineapple Log Cabin variation with two options for the center of the block: a square on-point, which echoes the corner lines, or a smaller square within that square on-point, which allows the fabric used for the diagonals to contrast with the center. The graphics of this pattern emerge best in multiples; we show the pattern with four blocks, in two different rotations.

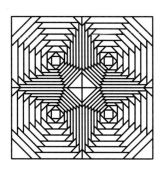 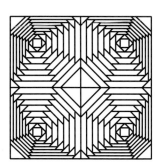

The Pineapple graphics depend on strong value contast between the diagonal strips and those on the horizontal-vertical planes. The geese in this pattern must be the darkest of the fabrics. It is important to mark your color choices on the foundation. The pattern has variables in both size and color within the same row and it is easy to become confused.

Directions:
1. Use quick-cutting techniques to cut strips for the logs. The geese can be made with strips or with squares cut diagonally.
2. Place the center square on the foundation and piece light strips around it for Row 1. You will be using two different widths of strips. Trim the seam allowances to a scant ¼"; ⅛" for the thinnest logs. In order to minimize distortion, piece on opposite sides of the center square for the first few rows.
3. Piece using dark strips for Row 2, including the geese. Continue piecing to the outside of the block, alternating light and dark rows. It is possible to pin and stitch two strips at one time, hopping from the end of one line to the beginning of the next.

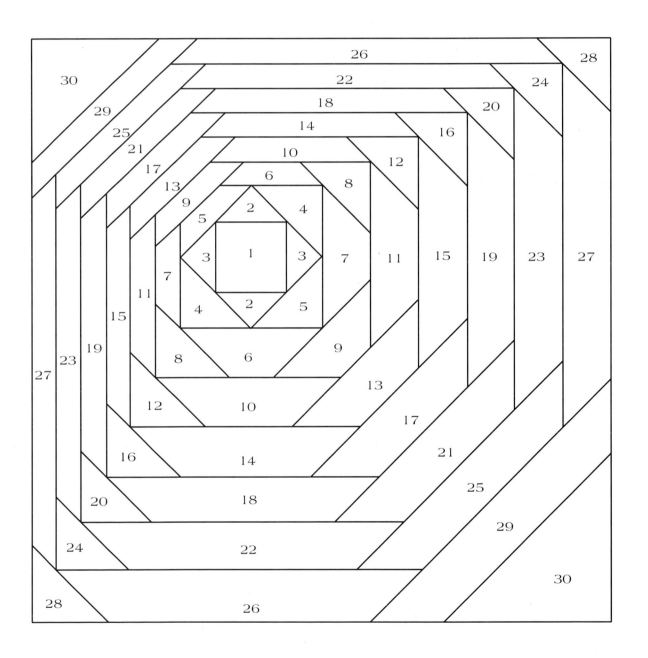

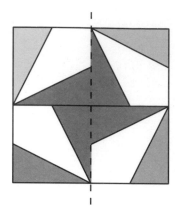

8

DIXIE'S STAR

Block Plate 12, Gallery Plates 10, 13

Size: 8"
Segments: 2
Piecing technique: *Under* pressed-piecing
Drafting category: Four-Patch (16 grid)

The corners of this block repeat the star when multiple blocks are joined. The pattern is pieced in two identical halves, with one rotated for block assembly. Be sure to mark the top of each foundation; if you reverse a foundation, you will have two identical sides. Use rough-cut templates to cut fabric for the patches.

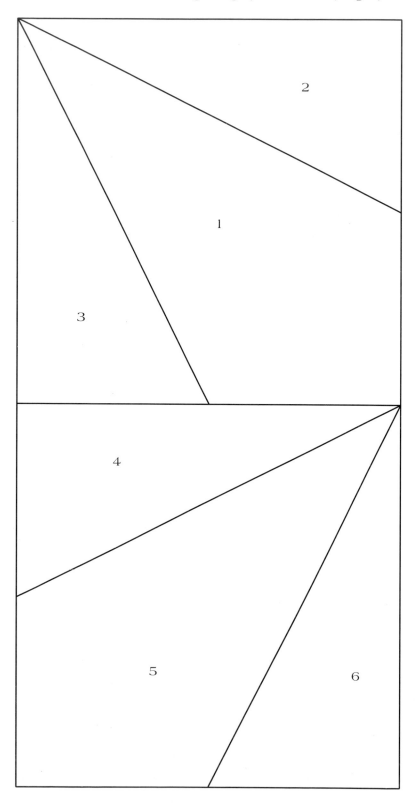

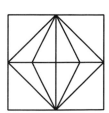

Chinese Lanterns

50

DUTCHMAN'S PUZZLE

Block Plates 13, 14

Size: 8"
Segments: 2
Piecing technique: *Under* pressed-piecing
Drafting category: Four-Patch (16 grid)

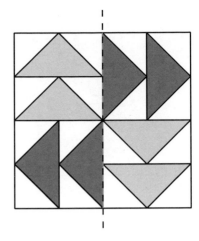

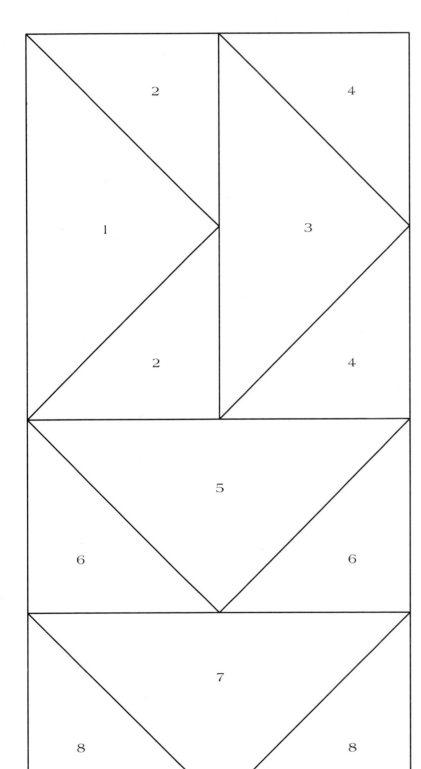

This pattern is pieced in two identical halves, with one rotated for block assembly. *Under* pressed-piecing the segment as drawn will result in a mirror-image design, producing the block as pictured. Be sure to mark the top of each foundation; if you reverse a foundation you will create two of the same side. It may be helpful to mark the piecing order on the foundations.

The two sizes of triangles must be cut differently to maintain the proper grainline. Use quick-cutting techniques for half-square and quarter-square triangles.

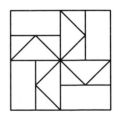

See Saw   Louisiana

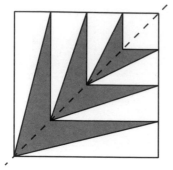

10

THE PALM

Block Plate 15

Size: 6"
Segments: 2
Piecing technique: *Under* pressed-
  piecing
Drafting category: Four-Patch (16
  grid)

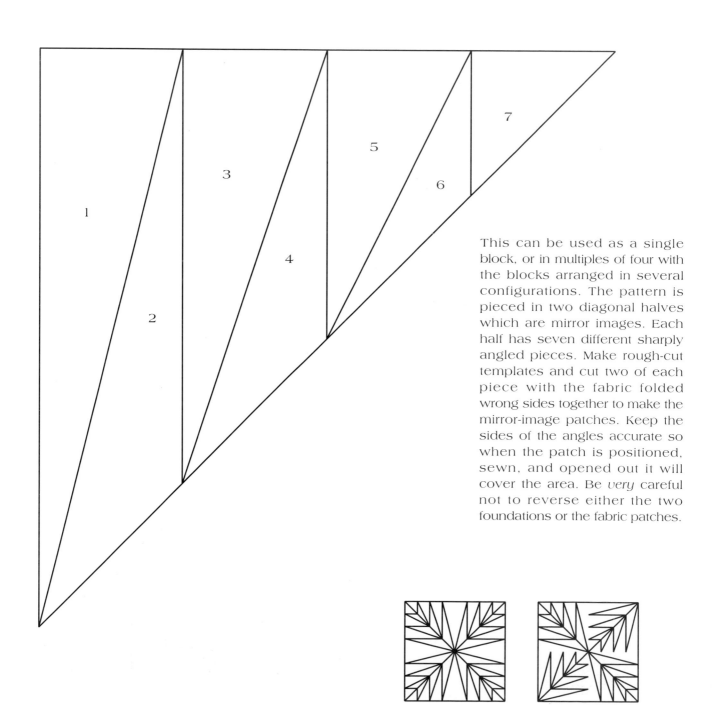

This can be used as a single block, or in multiples of four with the blocks arranged in several configurations. The pattern is pieced in two diagonal halves which are mirror images. Each half has seven different sharply angled pieces. Make rough-cut templates and cut two of each piece with the fabric folded wrong sides together to make the mirror-image patches. Keep the sides of the angles accurate so when the patch is positioned, sewn, and opened out it will cover the area. Be *very* careful not to reverse either the two foundations or the fabric patches.

4 Blocks   4 Blocks

FISH IN A DISH

Block Plates 16, 17

Size: 8"
Segments: 2
Piecing technique: *Under* pressed-
  piecing
Drafting category: Seven-patch (49
  grid)

11

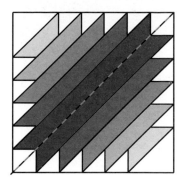

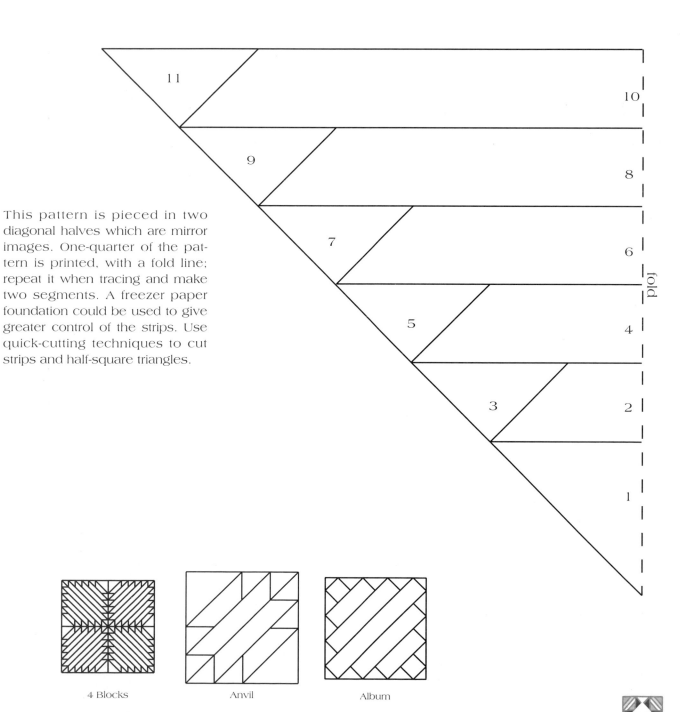

This pattern is pieced in two
diagonal halves which are mirror
images. One-quarter of the pattern is printed, with a fold line;
repeat it when tracing and make
two segments. A freezer paper
foundation could be used to give
greater control of the strips. Use
quick-cutting techniques to cut
strips and half-square triangles.

4 Blocks   Anvil   Album

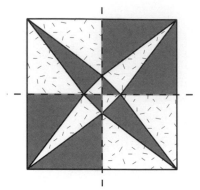

12

CROSSED CANOES
Block Plate 18

Size: 12"
Segments: 4
Piecing technique: *Under* pressed-
  piecing
Drafting category: Four-Patch

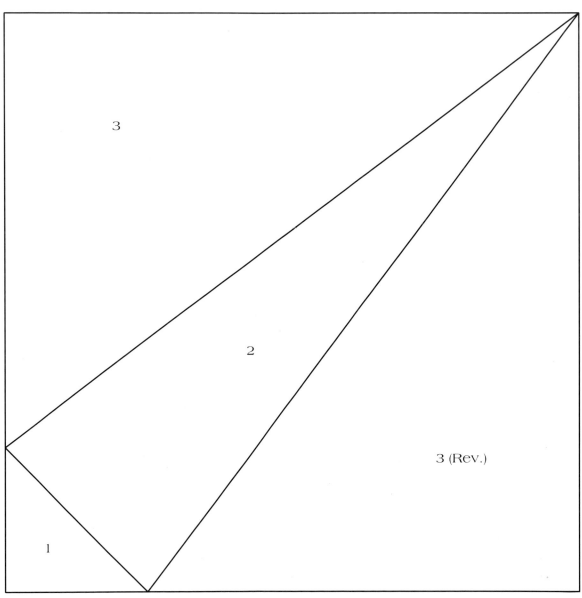

3

2

3 (Rev.)

1

Traditionally, four blocks of this pattern are rotated with pairs of alternating coloration. This is considered by some a whole block, but since it depends on multiples of four for its graphics, we have categorized it as a quarter block. Use rough-cut templates to cut fabric, and cut fabric for the large corner triangles wrong sides together to create mirror-image patches. Be aware that the large corner triangles are asymmetrical and check that you have positioned them correctly before stitching.

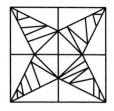

Rocky Road to Kansas

ELECTRIC STAR

Block Plate 19, Gallery Plate 17

Size: 12"

Segments: 4

Piecing technique: *Under* pressed-
 piecing

Drafting category: Crazy patch

13

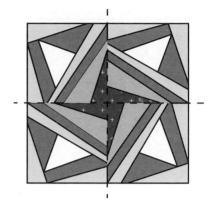

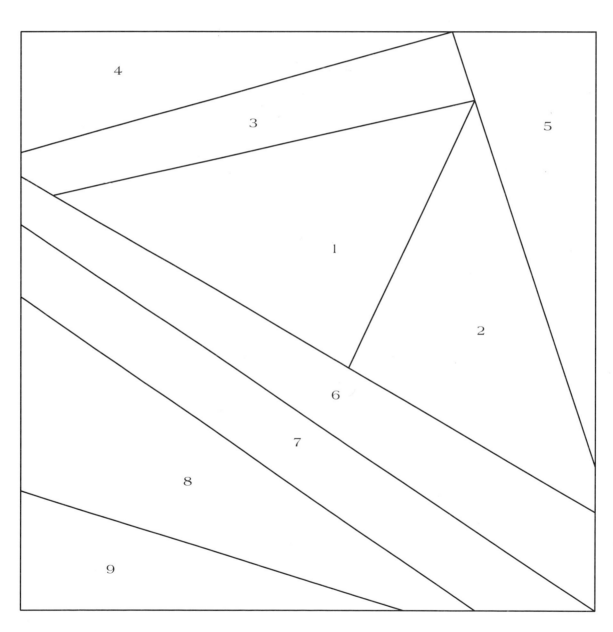

This was designed on a computer as a planned crazy patch. To create the star, four identical segments are rotated. There are other design possibilities, using a single segment or different combinations of segments.

PATTERNS
Quarter Blocks

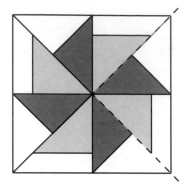

14

PINWHEEL
Block Plates 20, 21

Size: 8"
Segments: 4
Piecing technique: *Under* pressed-piecing
Drafting category: Four-Patch (64 grid)

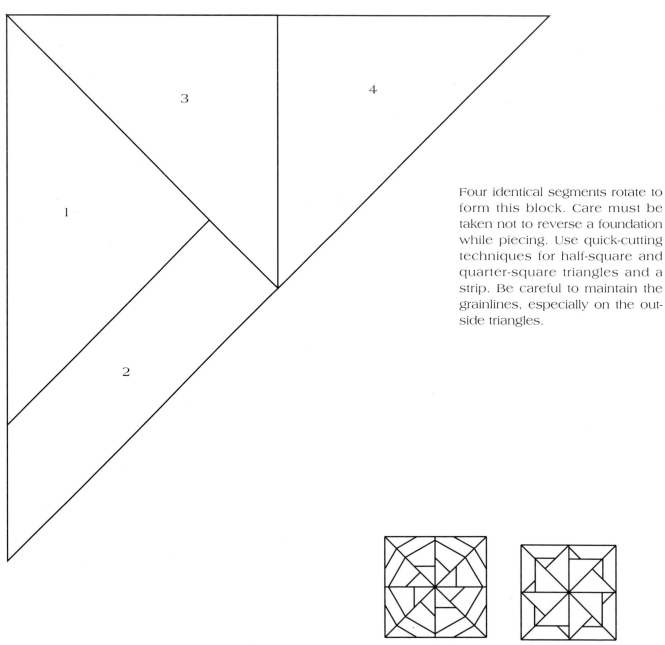

Four identical segments rotate to form this block. Care must be taken not to reverse a foundation while piecing. Use quick-cutting techniques for half-square and quarter-square triangles and a strip. Be careful to maintain the grainlines, especially on the outside triangles.

Wheel of Fortune   Spinning Color Wheel

15

STARRY PATH

Block Plates 22, 23

Size 8"

Segments: 4

Piecing technique: *Under* pressed-piecing

Drafting category: Four-Patch

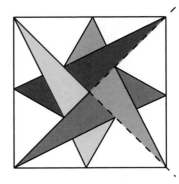

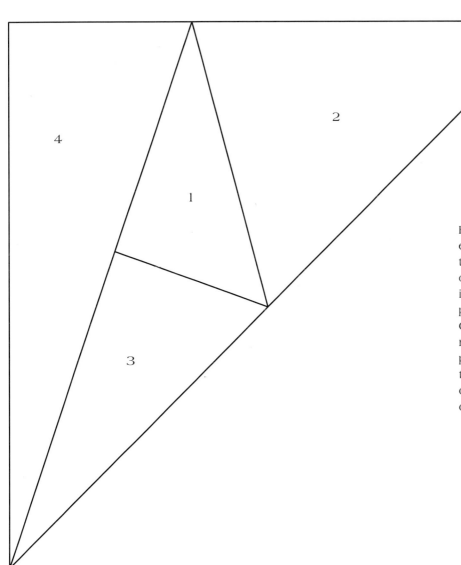

Four identical segments are rotated to form this block. It is important to mark the color placement on the foundation before cutting it into segments, especially when piecing the woven-star version. Care must be taken to avoid reversing the foundation while piecing. Use rough-cut templates to cut fabric. Press firmly and carefully to maintain the sharp corner points.

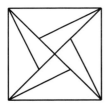

Wheel of Destiny

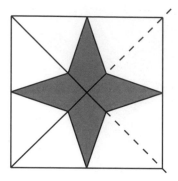

16

RUBY'S STAR

Block Plate 24

Size 8"

Segments: 4

Piecing techniques: *Top* and *under* pressed-piecing

Drafting category: Four-Patch

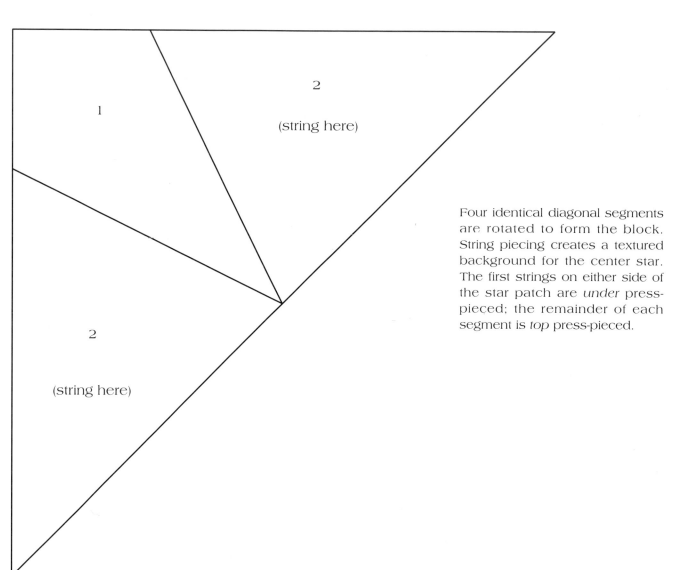

1

2

(string here)

2

(string here)

Four identical diagonal segments are rotated to form the block. String piecing creates a textured background for the center star. The first strings on either side of the star patch are *under* press-pieced; the remainder of each segment is *top* press-pieced.

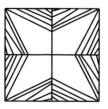
Stars and Stripes

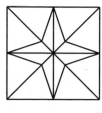
Telstar

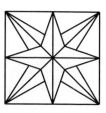
Blazing Star

KEY WEST BEAUTY

Block Plate 25

Size: 8"
Segments: 4
Piecing technique: *Under* pressed-
  piecing
Drafting category: Eight-pointed star

17

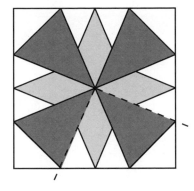

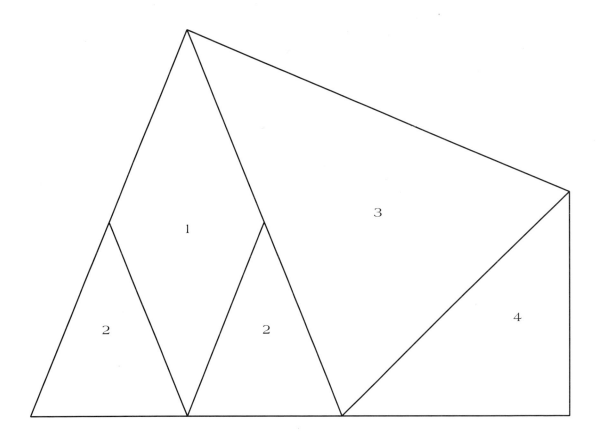

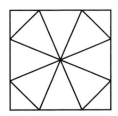

Kaleidoscope

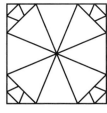

Arrowheads

This is in the kaleidoscope family of patterns. Four identical asymmetrical segments are rotated to form the block. Use rough-cut templates to cut the fabric patches.

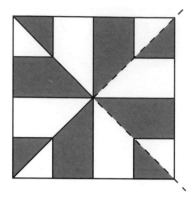

18

Size: 8"
Segments: 4
Piecing technique: *Under* pressed-
   piecing
Drafting category: Four-Patch

Four identical rotated segments form this block which creates an optical illusion of dimension with two alternating values. This is best pieced on freezer paper to control the fabric joins. There are two options for piecing the segments: you can piece them individually on four foundation segments, or you can strip piece a long strip set from which the segments will be cut (Ref p.19). By cutting the foundations without adding an outside seam allowance, the first option makes it possible to avoid having freezer paper in any seam allowance.

To use the second option, cut a piece of freezer paper 9" x 21". Draw parallel lines 2" apart, beginning ½" from one of the long sides. Make a template of the segment pattern and trace it four times on the freezer paper, allowing room for a ¼" seam allowance on all sides. Cut one strip each of dark and light fabric 2½" x 21", and one of each color 2¾" x 21". *Under* press-piece onto the freezer paper, alternating colors. Begin with the wider light strip and end with the wider dark strip. Press carefully after each seam, first from the fabric side and then from the paper side to avoid pleats at the seam line. Cut out the segments, adding ¼" seam allowance on all sides, and assemble the block.

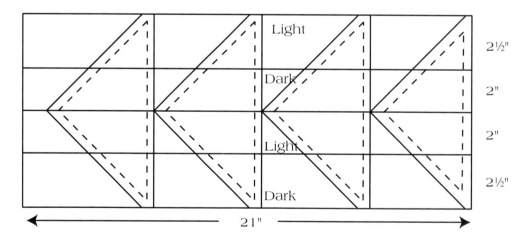

Diagram: segments on strip-set.

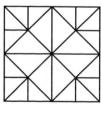

Windmill

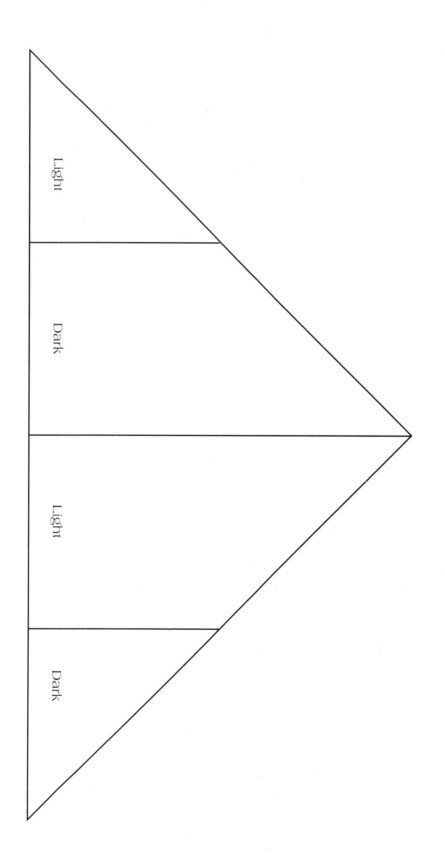

Light

Dark

Light

Dark

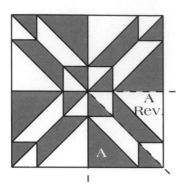

19

FEATHERBONE

Block Plate 27

Size: 8"

Segments: 8
Piecing technique: *Under* pressed-piecing
Drafting category: Nine-Patch (36 grid)

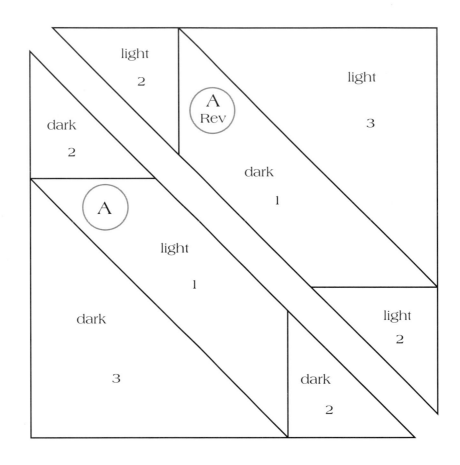

This block has four identical pairs of mirror-image segments. The optical illusion of the block is caused by the fact that the color also is arranged in mirror images. It is incredibly easy to reverse the foundation segments or the color placement. We suggest that you mark the foundations with the colors, which will also indicate the top side, before cutting them into segments. Use quick-cutting techniques to cut fabric for the half-square triangles and strips. Lay out all the pieced segments in the block configuration before piecing because your eye will not read "star" as you assemble them, and it is easy to become confused and turn the segments upside down.

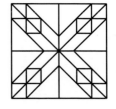

Patch as Patch Can

20

ST. LOUIS STAR

Block Plates 28, 29

Size: 8"

Segments: 8

Piecing technique: *Under* pressed-
piecing

Drafting category: Four-Patch (64
grid)

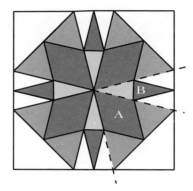

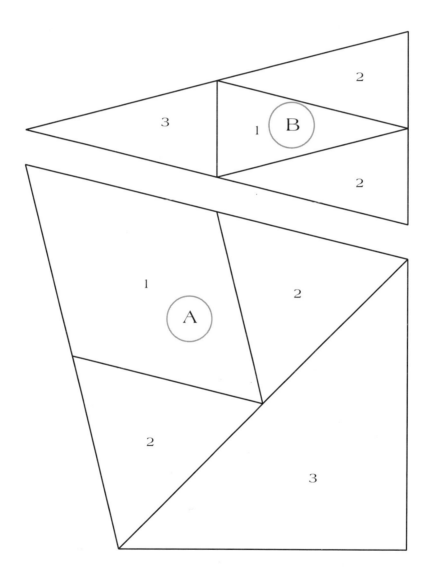

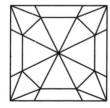

Joseph's Coat

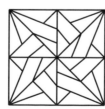

Tangled Star Variation

This block has two different segments, each
repeated four times. Use rough-cut templates to
cut the fabrics for all the patches. Be careful to cut
the fabric angles for the triangles exactly, both to
retain a consistent grainline and to cover the
spaces.

63

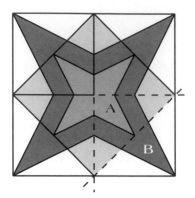

21

BEGINNER'S STAR

Block Plates 31, 32

Size: 8"
Segments: 8
Piecing technique: *Under* pressed-
    piecing
Drafting category: Four-Patch (64 grid)

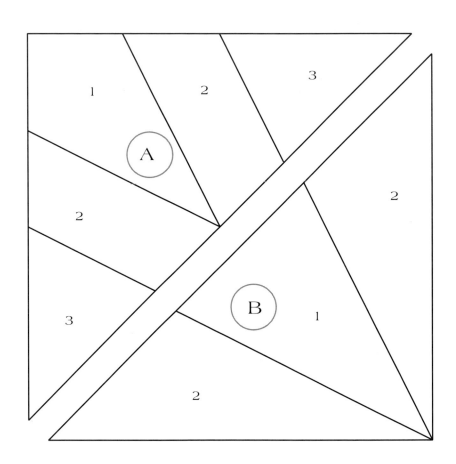

This rare pattern was first published by Jan Halgrimson in *Scraps Can Be Beautiful*. The block has two pairs of segments, each repeated four times. Most of the pieces in each segment are mirror images and need to be cut from rough-cut templates with the fabric wrong sides together. The pattern is unusual in that it does not have eight points joining in the middle. The final joining seam has seven matching points, which more than makes up for the fact that the center is a simple one.

BROKEN STAR

Block Plate 30

Size 8"

Segments: 5

Piecing technique: *Under* pressed-
piecing

Drafting category: Four-Patch (64
grid)

22

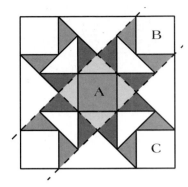

This block has three different segments, one of A, and two each of
B and C. Use quick-cutting techniques to cut the half- and quarter-
square triangles, keeping the
grainline consistent.

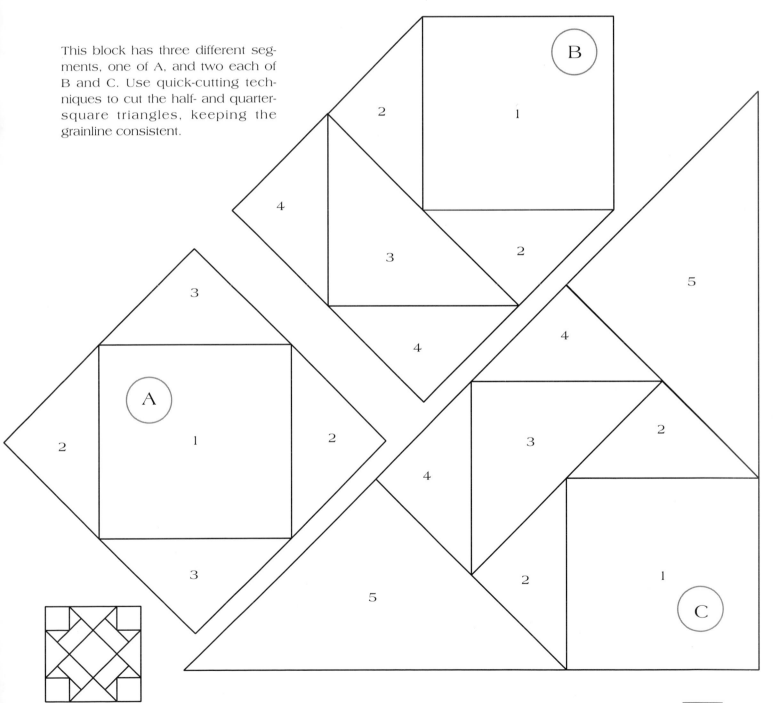

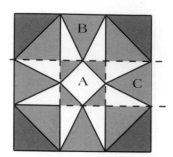

23

GULF STAR

Block Plate 33, Gallery Plate 3

Size: 8"

Segments: 5

Piecing technique: *Under* pressed-piecing

Drafting category: Nine-Patch (36 grid)

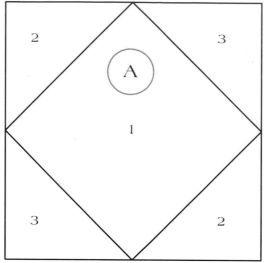

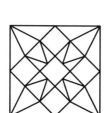

Dog Tooth Violet

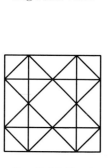

Four Patch Fox & Geese

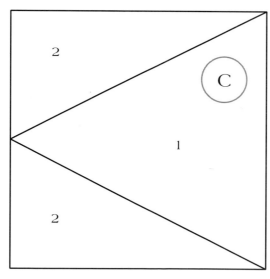

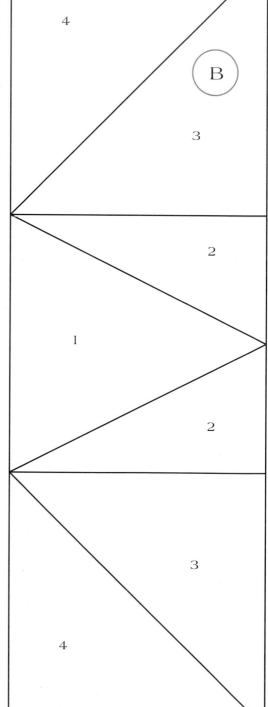

This block has three different segments, one of A and two each of B and C. We suggest using quick-cutting techniques to cut the half-square triangles and using rough-cut templates to cut the remaining patches.

24

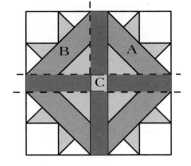

MEXICAN STAR

Block Plate 34

Size: 8"

Segments: 5

Piecing technique: *Under* pressed-piecing

Drafting category: Nine-Patch (81 grid)

fold

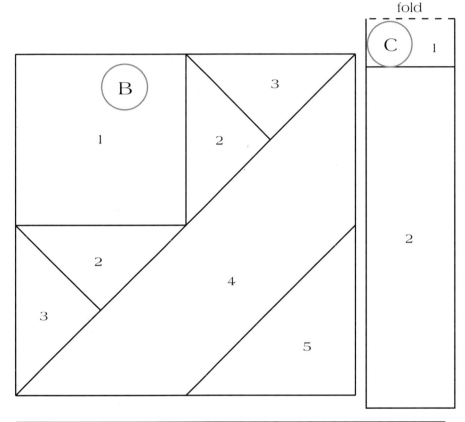

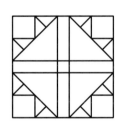

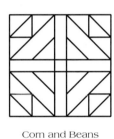

Corn and Beans

Cross and Crown

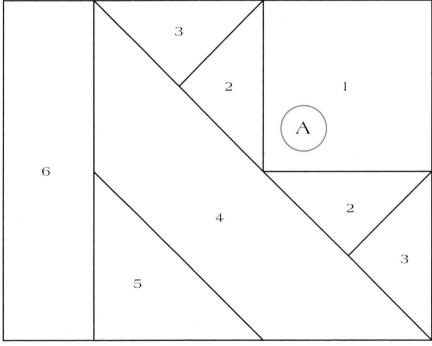

This block has three different segments, two each of A and B, and one of C, which is printed with a fold line; repeat the other half when drawing the foundation. We recommend freezer paper be used for the C foundation, to control the long, unsecured strips. Use quick-cutting techniques to cut the half- and quarter-square triangles, keeping the grainline consistent.

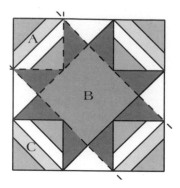

25

NIGHT AND NOON

Block Plates 35, 36

Size: 8"

Segments: 4

Piecing technique: *Under* pressed-
piecing

Drafting category: Nine-Patch (36
grid)

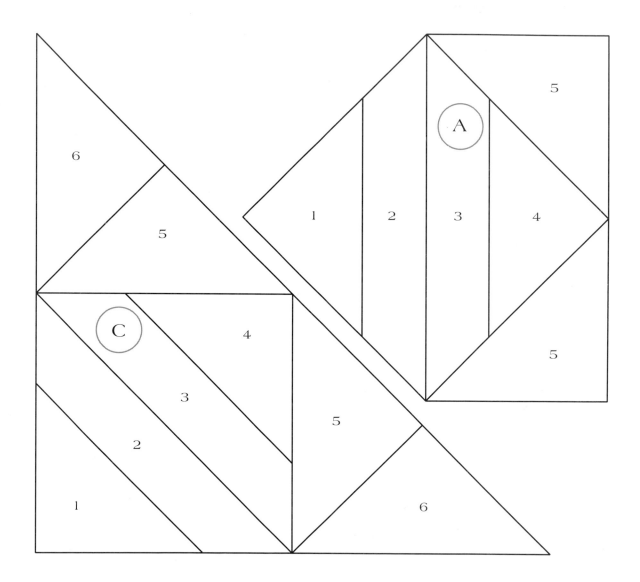

This block creates interesting secondary designs when multiples are joined. It has three different segments, one each of A and B, and two of C. Use quick-cutting techniques for strips and quarter-square triangles.

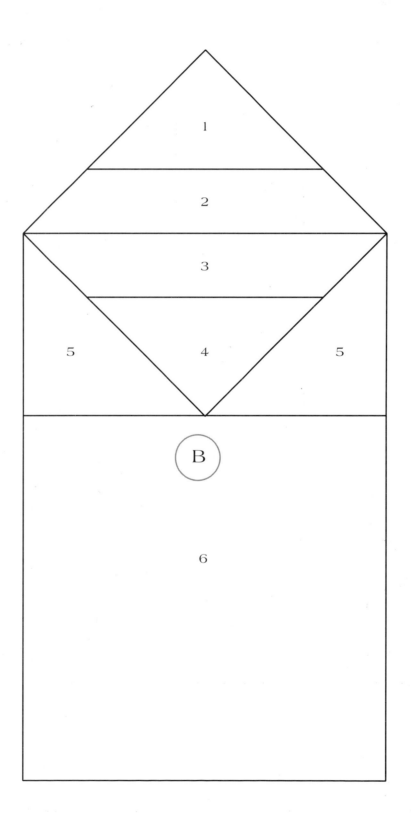

26

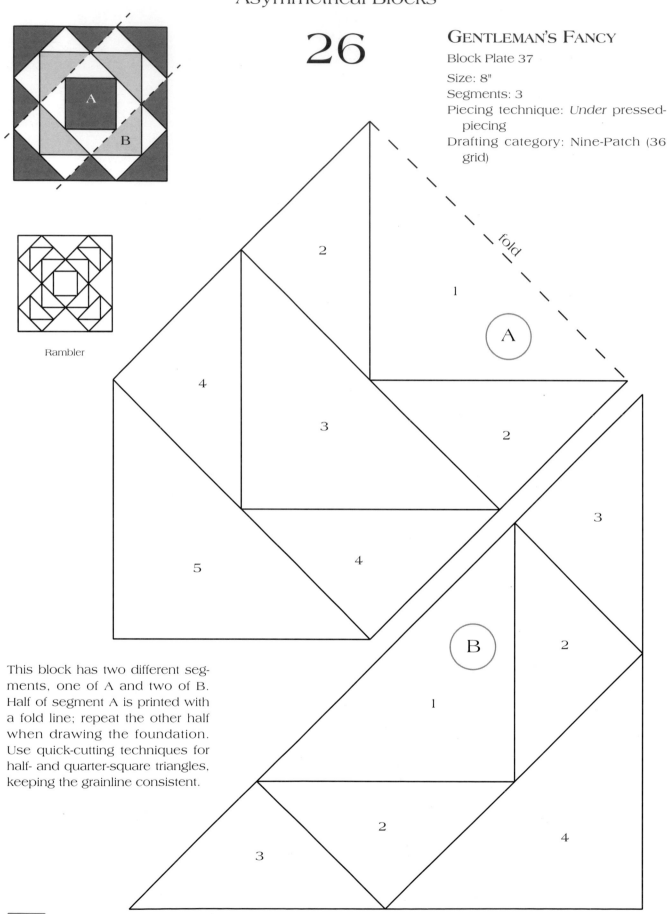

GENTLEMAN'S FANCY

Block Plate 37

Size: 8"

Segments: 3

Piecing technique: *Under* pressed-piecing

Drafting category: Nine-Patch (36 grid)

Rambler

This block has two different segments, one of A and two of B. Half of segment A is printed with a fold line; repeat the other half when drawing the foundation. Use quick-cutting techniques for half- and quarter-square triangles, keeping the grainline consistent.

JACK IN THE PULPIT

Block Plate 38, Gallery Plate 30

Size: 8"

Segments: 5

Piecing technique: *Under* pressed-
  piecing

Drafting category: Four-Patch, with
  Nine-Patch overlay.

27

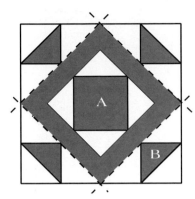

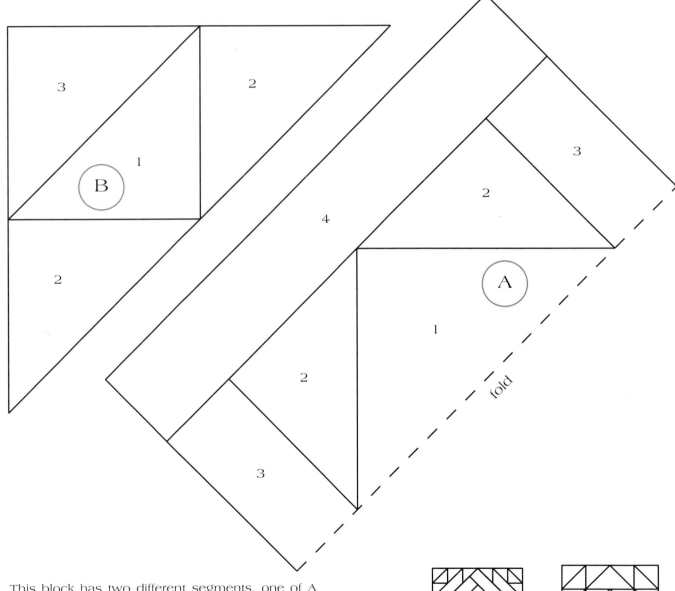

This block has two different segments, one of A
and four of B. Half of segment A is printed with a
fold line; repeat the other half when drawing the
foundation. Use quick-cutting techniques for strips
and half-square triangles.

Mother's Favorite

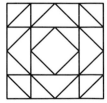

Connecticut

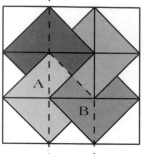

28

CARD TRICK

Block Plate 39

Size: 8"

Segments: 4

Piecing technique: *Under* pressed-piecing

Drafting category: Nine-Patch (36 grid)

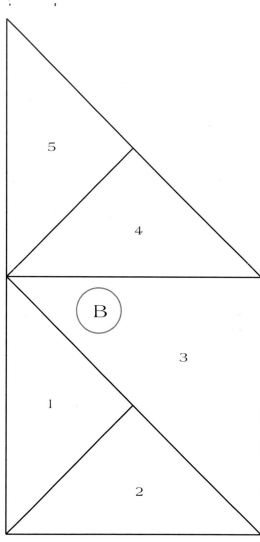

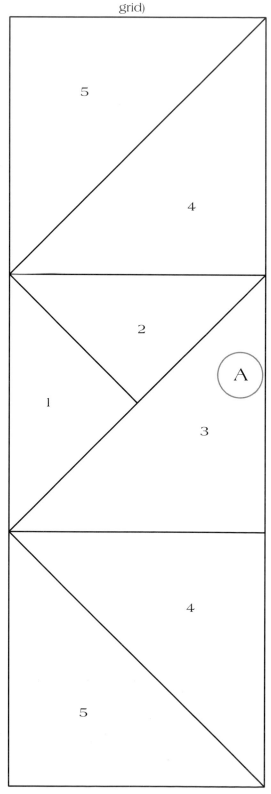

This block has two different segments each repeated twice. To avoid confusion, it is essential to write color choices on the foundation before the segments are cut apart, and to lay out the fabric patches as they will be pieced. Use quick-cutting techniques for half- and quarter-square triangles, keeping the grainline consistent.

PATTERNS
Asymmetrical Blocks

29

FRIENDSHIP WEAVE

Block Plate 40

Size: 8"

Segments: 3

Piecing technique: *Under* pressed-
 piecing

Drafting category: Nine-Patch (36
 grid)

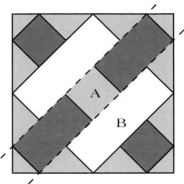

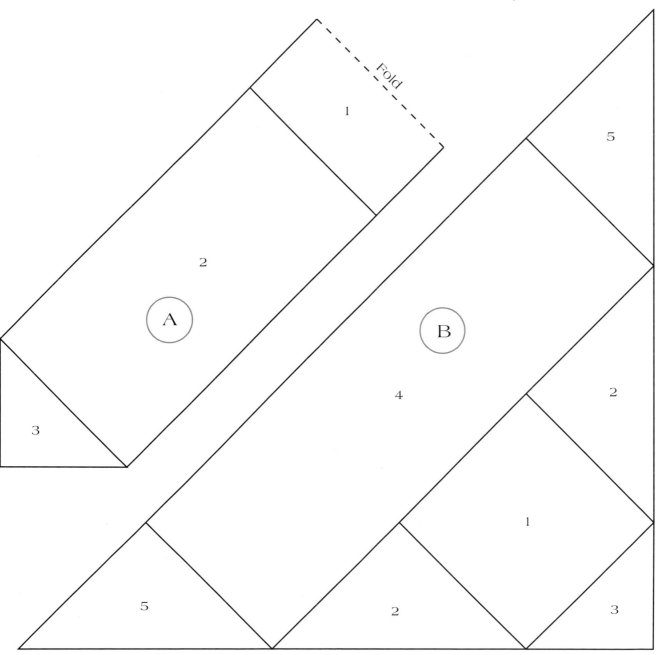

This block has two different segments, one of A and two of B. Half of segment A is printed with a fold line; repeat the other half when drawing the block. Use quick-cutting techniques for strips and quarter-square triangles.

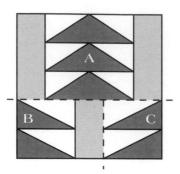

30

TALL PINE TREE

Block Plate 41

Size: 8"

Segments: 3

Piecing technique: *Under* pressed-
piecing

Drafting category: Five-patch

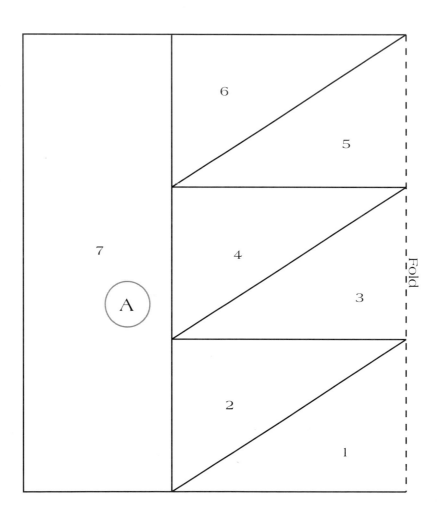

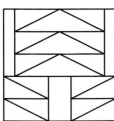

Tall Pine Variation

Multiples of this block create secondary designs that repeat the tree motif. The variation makes the same size trunks and treetops when used in multiples.

The block has three different segments, each used once. Segment A is printed with a fold line; repeat the other half when drawing the foundation. Use rough-cut templates to cut fabric so the grainline is correct and the sharp angled patches cover the area.

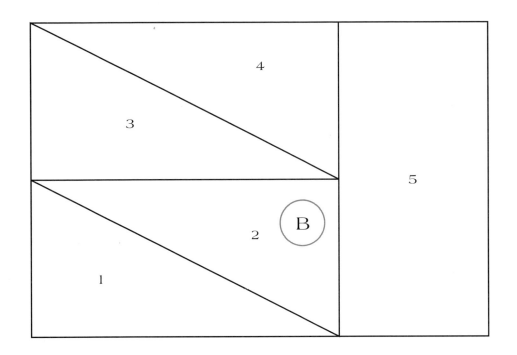

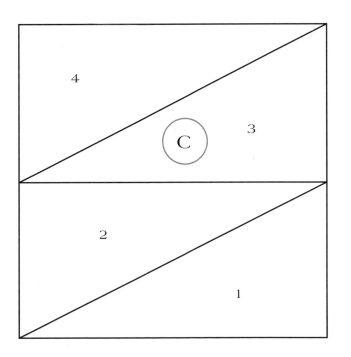

31

WILD GOOSE CHASE
(variation)

Block Plate 42

Size: 8"
Segments: 3
Piecing technique: *Under* pressed-piecing
Drafting category: Four-Patch (64 grid)

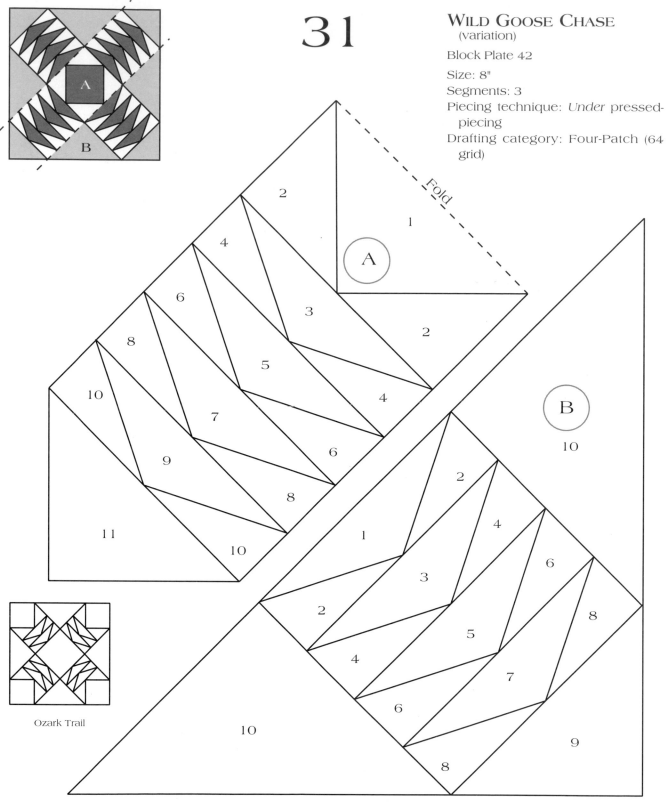

Ozark Trail

This block has two different segments, one of A and two of B. Half of segment A is printed with a fold line; repeat the other half when drawing the segment. Quick-cut the fabric where possible with half- and quarter-square triangles, keeping the grainline consistent. Use rough-cut templates for the fabric for the geese and their setting triangles, placing the straight grain on the long side of the geese. It is very important to cut the sides of the angles correctly and, after stitching, to trim the seam allowances accurately before positioning the next piece. Slim, angled pieces are easily skewed and then won't cover the space when pressed open.

PATTERNS
Asymmetrical Blocks

BUTTERFLY
Block Plates 43, 44

Size: 8"
Segments: 4
Piecing technique: *Under* pressed-
  piecing
Drafting category: Five-patch

32

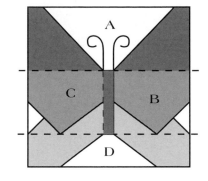

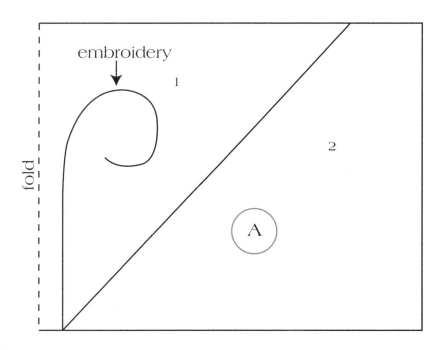

This block has four different segments, each used once. Segments A and D are each printed
with a fold line; repeat the other
half when drawing the foundation. Use embroidery for the
antennae.

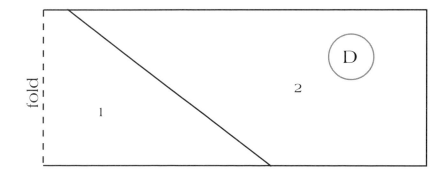

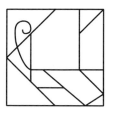

Butterfly #2

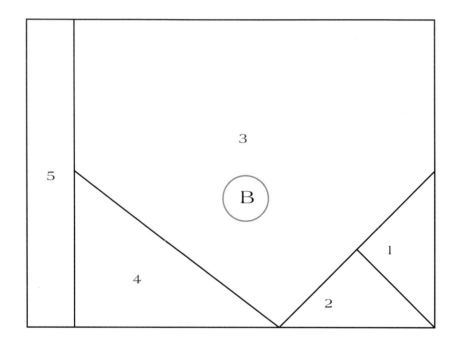

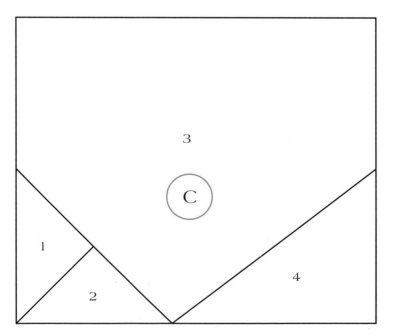

EIGHT-POINTED STAR

Block Plate 45, Gallery Plate 4

Size: 8"
Segments: 16
Piecing technique: Single founda-
   tion piecing
Drafting category: Eight-pointed star

33

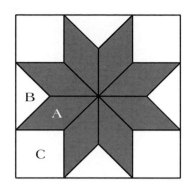

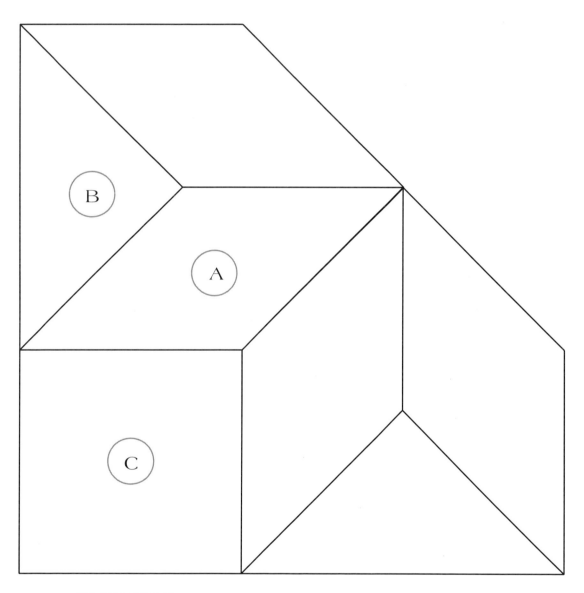

Liberty Star

Draw the complete block onto freezer paper, extrapolating from the portion given. Cut apart into single foundations and press each onto the wrong side of fabrics.

33

Lay out the segments as they will be pieced in the pattern, and stitch a square or a triangle background piece alternately onto the same side of each diamond, keeping the laid-out order. Diagram 1.

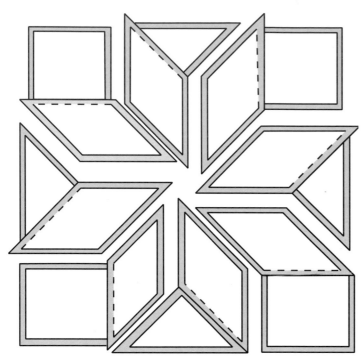

Diagram 1: Initial stitching.

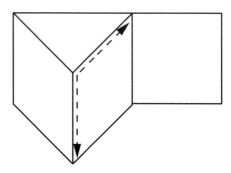

Diagram 2: Joining segments.

Stitch two segments together in two steps, sewing out from the middle section of the diamonds. Stitch from point to point only, keeping the seam allowances free and backstitching at the beginning of the line. Diagram 2.

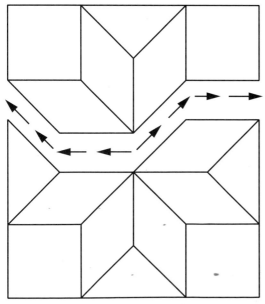

Diagram 3: Final assembly.

The center of an Eight-Pointed Star can create problems with eight lines of stitching and all the seam allowances coming to a single point. We use a method proposed by Erma Kirkpatrick from Chapel Hill, NC, who stitches the diamonds together to form units of 3 and 5 points. Set the three diamond piece into the five diamond piece, sewing in two steps as before, from the center out. Setting in these wide angles is an easier task than the traditional right-angle set-in for this pattern. Diagram 3.

MOSAIC

Block Plates 46, 47

Size: 8"
Segments: 25
Piecing technique: Single founda-
   tion piecing
Drafting category: Hexagon grid

34

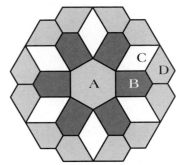

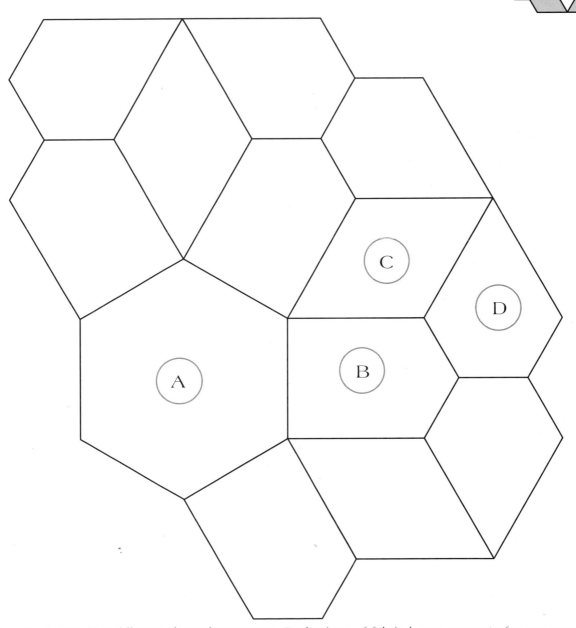

The block has four different shaped segments. Each piece of fabric has a separate freezer paper foundation and is set into the pattern. There are two ways you can prepare the foundations. The first is to trace a complete pattern onto freezer paper, extrapolating from the pattern portion given. You may also draw the foundations individually, cutting one of #A, six each of #B and #C, and twelve of #D. Cut out the single foundations and press them to the wrong side of the fabrics. Cut the fabric with a ¼" seam allowance on all sides and sew by hand, machine, or a combination of both. Be careful not to extend the stitching beyond the foundation corners into the seam allowance or you will be unable to set in subsequent pieces. The block can be appliquéd to a background, or the outside row can act as a joining row for repeats of the center design.

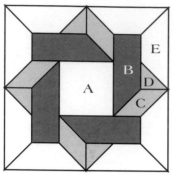

35

INTERLOCKED SQUARES

Block Plate 48

Size: 8"
Segments: 17
Piecing technique: Single founda-
    tion piecing
Drafting category: Nine-Patch (36
    grid)

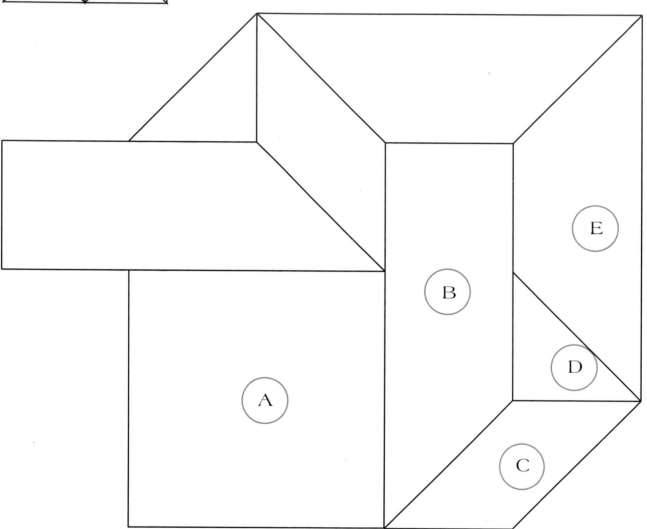

Trace the complete pattern onto freezer paper extrapolating from the
portion given. Mark your fabric choices on the freezer paper before cutting into single foundations and ironing it onto the wrong side of fabrics. Lay out the segments in the order in which they will be pieced in
the pattern. This block is virtually all set-in seams, and can be divided
for piecing in several different ways. We suggest you piece the four
corners and set them around the square so you can set in wide angles
rather than right angles.

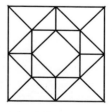

Windblown Square

FIELD OF DAISIES

Block Plate 49

Size: 8"
Segments: 12
Piecing technique: Single founda-
 tion piecing
Drafting category: Pictorial

36

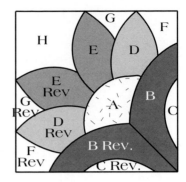

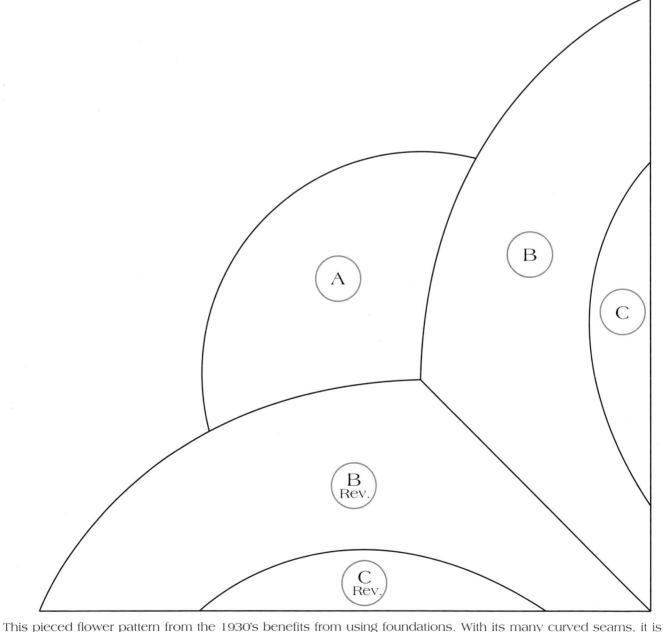

This pieced flower pattern from the 1930's benefits from using foundations. With its many curved seams, it is most easily pieced by hand. Trace the pattern onto freezer or adhesive paper, extrapolating from the portions given. One section is printed with a fold line; repeat the other half when drawing the foundation. Mark your color choices on the foundation, cut it apart into single foundations, and attach the foundations onto the wrong side of fabrics with ¼" seam allowances on all sides. Multiples of this pattern create a secondary design.

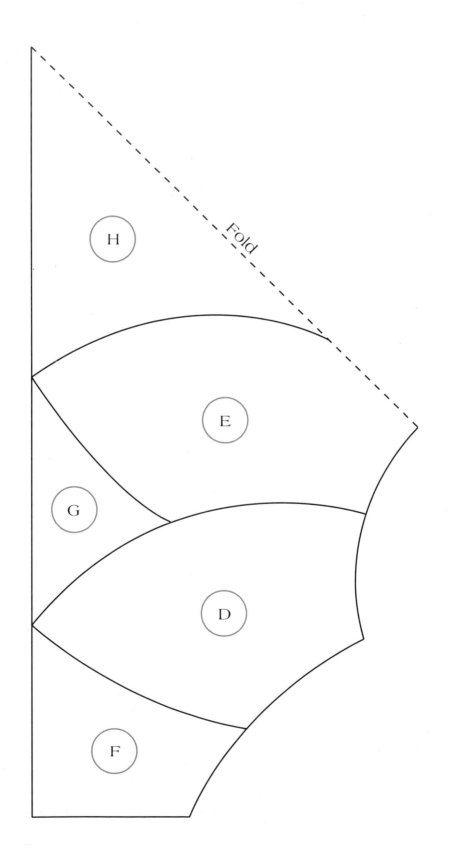

FLAT IRON

Block Plate 65

Size: 6" base

Segments: 4

Piecing techniques: *Under* pressed-
  piecing, single foundation piecing

Drafting category: Triangle

37

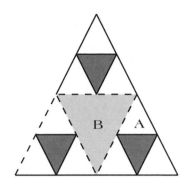

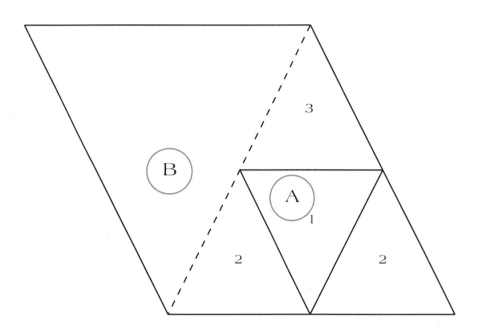

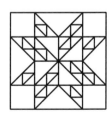

Twinkling Star

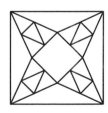

Signal Lights

This block is always used in multiples; we show three units set with a large triangle in the color plate. There are three press-pieced segments A and one single foundation segment B in each unit. Freezer paper is a good foundation for this pattern and its many variations because it controls the bias edges of the triangles. Be aware that the triangles are not equilateral; the base is a different length than the sides. Trace the pattern onto freezer paper and mark the grainline on each triangle. Cut it into segments, and press the single foundation onto the wrong side of fabric. Use rough-cut templates to cut the fabric for the press-pieced triangles.

38

EMERALD

Block Plates 50, 51

Size: 8"

Segments: 13

Piecing techniques: *Under* pressed-piecing, single foundation piecing

Drafting category: Nine-Patch (36 grid)

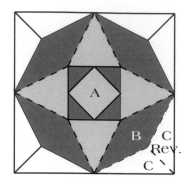

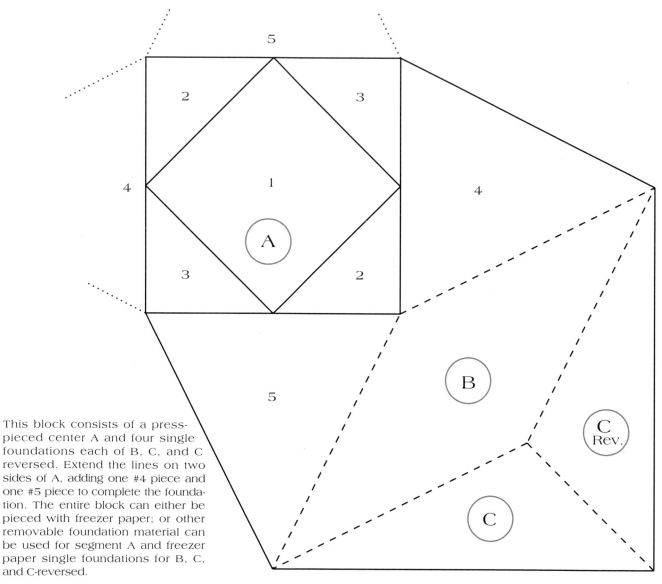

This block consists of a press-pieced center A and four single foundations each of B, C, and C reversed. Extend the lines on two sides of A, adding one #4 piece and one #5 piece to complete the foundation. The entire block can either be pieced with freezer paper; or other removable foundation material can be used for segment A and freezer paper single foundations for B, C, and C-reversed.

The single foundations are set into the center segment. When you press-piece segment A, be careful to not stitch into the seam allowances when adding #4 and #5.

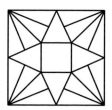

Exploding Star

PATTERNS
COMBINATION BLOCKS

39

SHEEP SAFELY GRAZING

Block Plate 52

Size: 6"

Segments: 6

Piecing techniques: *Under* pressed-piecing, single foundation piecing

Drafting category: Pictorial

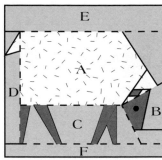

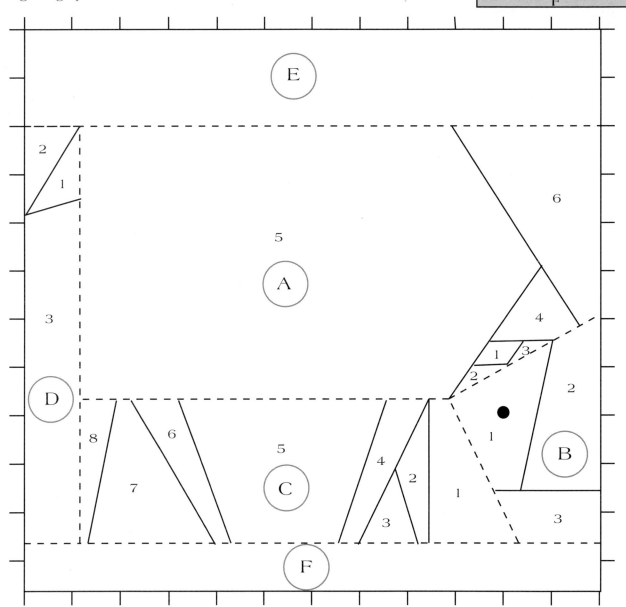

This pattern came from *Creature Comforts* by Barbara Brackman and Marie Shirer. We show it as they printed it, with grid marks for enlarging around the outside edge. It also can be enlarged on a copy machine. The pattern has a mirror image. If you wish the sheep to face as shown in the drawing, you must reverse the foundation (Ref p. 26). Trace the pattern twice, once on freezer paper for the foundations and once on plain paper for rough-cut templates. Transfer the piecing order to both tracings and mark the grainline on the rough-cut pattern. This block may be pieced completely with single foundations or may be divided into press-pieced and single segments as we have indicated on the pattern.

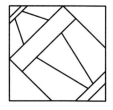

House   Airplane

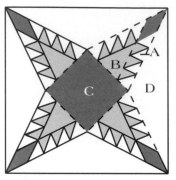

40

PINE BURR #1
Block Plate 53

Size: 8"
Segments: 13
Piecing techniques: *Under* pressed-
   piecing, single foundation piecing
Drafting category: Four-Patch

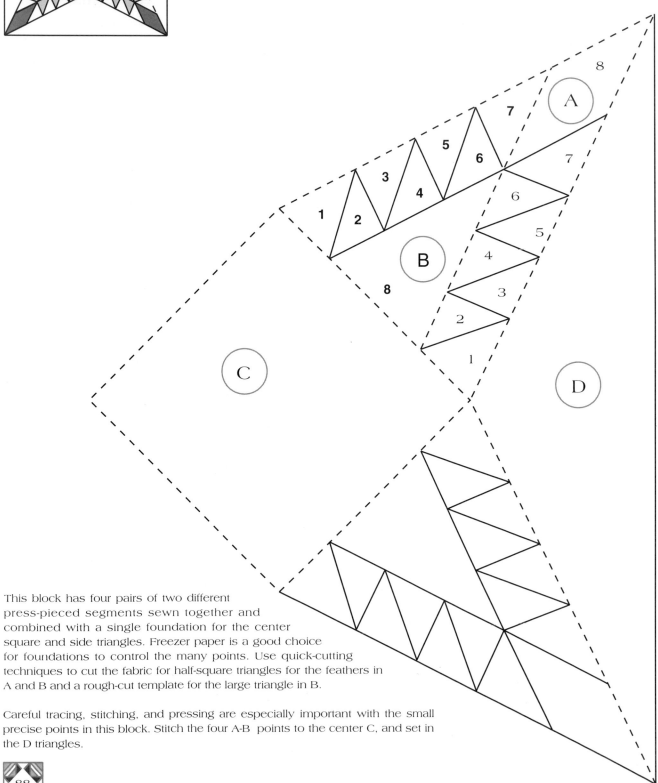

This block has four pairs of two different
press-pieced segments sewn together and
combined with a single foundation for the center
square and side triangles. Freezer paper is a good choice
for foundations to control the many points. Use quick-cutting
techniques to cut the fabric for half-square triangles for the feathers in
A and B and a rough-cut template for the large triangle in B.

Careful tracing, stitching, and pressing are especially important with the small
precise points in this block. Stitch the four A-B points to the center C, and set in
the D triangles.

PINE BURR #2

Block Plate 54, Gallery Plate 31

Size: 12"

Segments: 13

Piecing techniques: *Under* pressed-
   piecing, single foundation piecing,
   conventional piecing

Drafting category: Four-Patch

41

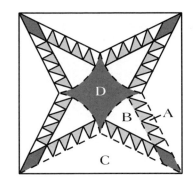

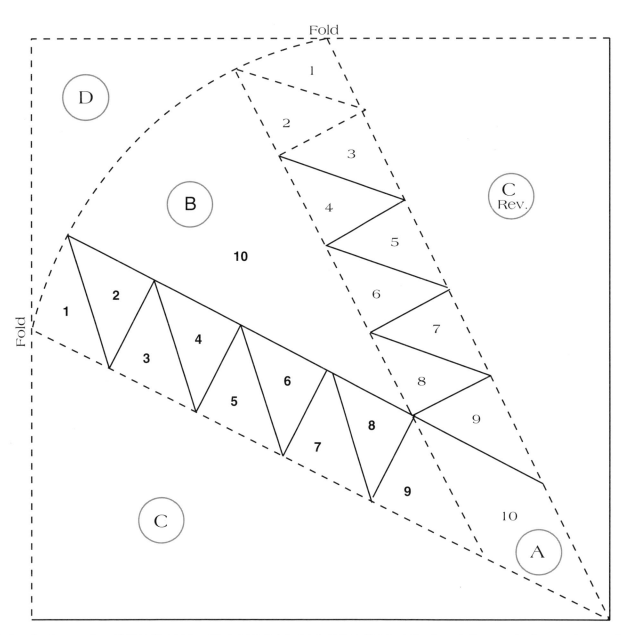

This is a larger version of Pine Burr #1, with a graceful curved center. Prepare the foundations as in the previous pattern, adding registration marks on the curved seams to ensure even placement. Press-piece segments A and B, taking care to maintain the sharp points.

The center is easiest to sew in place with conventional piecing, rather than backing it with inflexible freezer paper. Make a template for the center and trace around it to provide a sewing line, transferring the registration marks. Sew the points to the center and set in the side triangles.

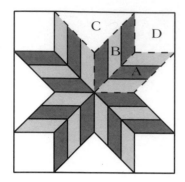

42

CROSSROADS
Block Plate 55

Size: 8"
Segments: 16
Piecing techniques: *Under* pressed-piecing, single foundation piecing
Drafting category: Four-Patch (16 grid)

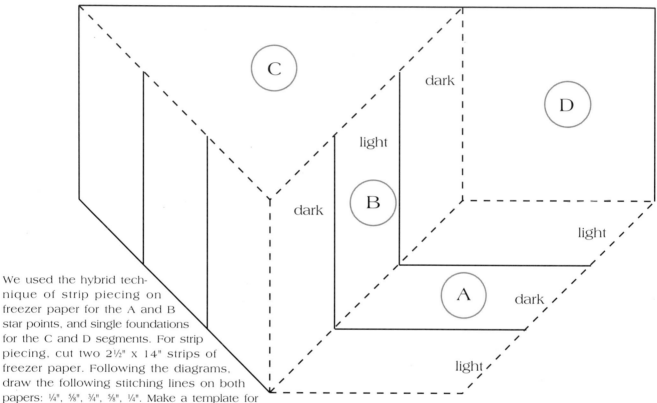

We used the hybrid technique of strip piecing on freezer paper for the A and B star points, and single foundations for the C and D segments. For strip piecing, cut two 2½" x 14" strips of freezer paper. Following the diagrams, draw the following stitching lines on both papers: ¼", ⅝", ¾", ⅝", ¼". Make a template for the parallelogram star point and trace it four times on each foundation, leaving at least ½" between each figure. The parallelograms on one foundation should be reversed from those on the other.

Piece strips of light and dark fabric on the two foundations, using *under* pressed-piecing. On foundation #1, sew light-dark-light strips; on foundation #2 sew dark-light-dark strips. Press carefully to avoid pleats. Cut out the parallelograms, adding a ¼" seam allowance on all sides. Arrange the segments, alternating units from foundation #1 and foundation #2. We like to add the set-in squares and triangles and assemble as shown in the Eight-Pointed Star (Ref Block 33, p. 79 – 80).

It is also possible to string piece on individual A and B foundations, taking care to retain the pattern orientation.

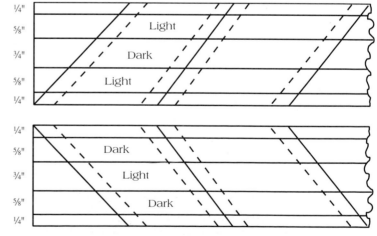

Diagram: Strip-set foundations for A & B segments.

43

FAN QUADRILLE

Block Plates 56, 57

Size: 12"

Segments: 5

Piecing techniques: *Under* pressed-
  piecing, conventional piecing

Drafting category: Four-Patch,
  curves

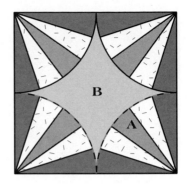

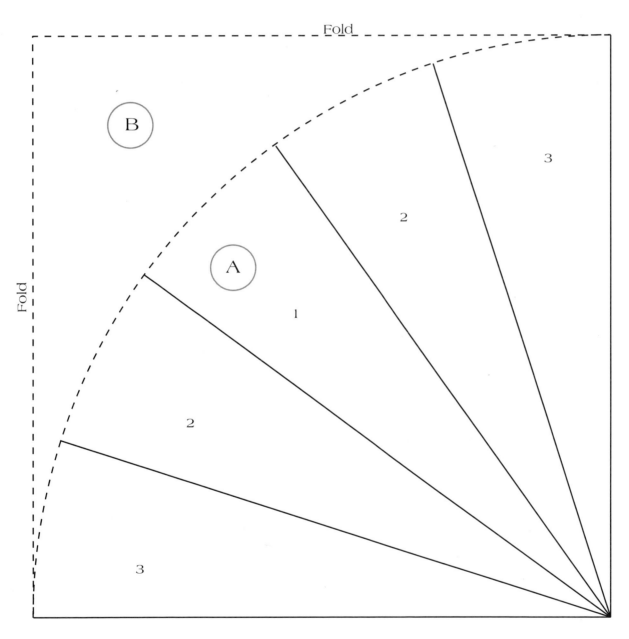

The block is constructed with four press-pieced fan segments A and a center B. One-quarter of the block is printed with a fold line; repeat four times when drawing the block. Add registration marks on the curved lines to make construction easy. The center is easiest to sew in place with conventional piecing, rather than backing it with inflexible freezer paper. Make a template for the center and trace around it to provide a sewing line, transferring the registration marks.

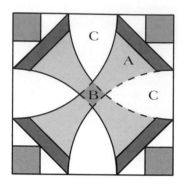

44

RALEIGH

Block Plate 58

Size: 8"
Segments: 9
Piecing techniques: *Under* pressed-
piecing, single foundation piec-
ing, conventional piecing
Drafting category: Curves

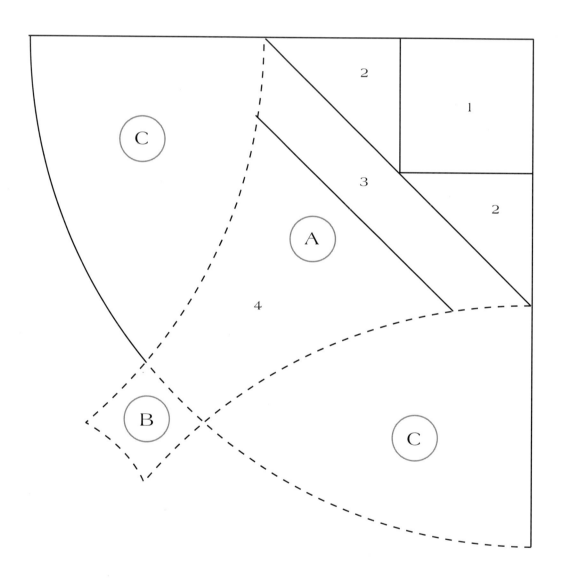

This block has four press-pieced segments A, one single foundation B, and four conventional segments C. Because of the curves, we used lightweight removable interfacing, which has some flexibility, for the press-pieced units. The curved C units are most easily pieced by marking a sewing line and registration marks with a template and then sewing in a conventional manner. Using freezer paper for single foundation B makes sewing easy along that small, gentle curve.

It is possible, with great care, to press-piece two C units onto either side of two A units and press-piece A-B-A. If you wish to attempt this method, use freezer paper for the A-B-A segment to control the long edges of the fabric and interfacing for the C-A-C units to give slight flexibility to the process.

LETHA'S ELECTRIC FAN

Block Plates 59, 60

Size: 12"

Segments: 13

Piecing techniques: *Under* pressed-
   piecing, conventional piecing,
   appliqué

Drafting category: Five-patch grid
   with curves

45

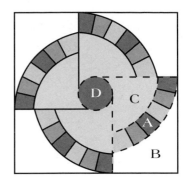

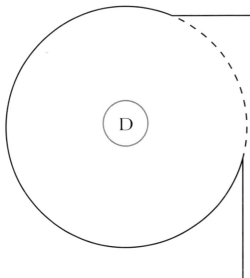

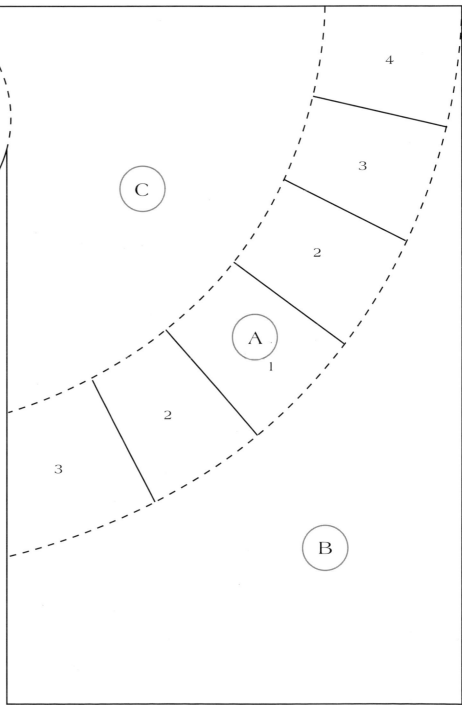

The printed pattern is one quarter of the block with the center added. This block has four press-pieced arcs A and four each of conventional segments B and C. By starting in the center of the arc and piecing outward in both directions, it can be chain pieced, pressing and trimming efficiently. Make templates for B and C, marking sewing lines and transferring registration marks on the curves. The center is appliquéd after the block is assembled.

MARINER'S COMPASS

Block Plates 61, 62

Gallery Plates 19, 20

Sizes: 8", 4", 3"

Segments: 8" and 4" compasses - 17;
  3" compass - 8.

Piecing techniques: *Under* pressed-
  piecing, single foundation piecing,
  appliqué

Drafting category: Mariner's Compass

46, 47 & 48

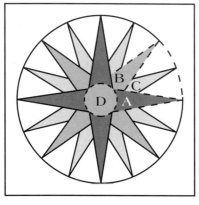

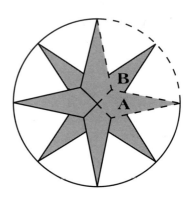

I   II   III

Compass	Single foundation segments	Press-pieced segments	Center
8"	four A, four B	eight C	D
4"	four A, four B	eight C	D
3"	four A	four B	

Because of the need to control the many points, we recommend freezer paper foundations for both the press-pieced and the single-foundation segments. The 8" compass is printed as a half section; draw the complete block, extrapolating from the portion given. Trace the patterns onto the dull side of freezer paper, mark your color choices on the foundation, and cut it into segments. Use rough-cut templates to cut fabric for press piecing. Press baste the fabric for point B (3" compass) or point C (4" and 8" compasses) onto the foundation by touching it to the shiny side of the freezer paper with the tip of a hot iron. Complete the press-piecing and assemble the block, matching all points and checking that the outer arc is even. Trim the seams to a scant ¼", tapering to ⅛" at the outer compass tips.

The two small compasses are not set into squares although they could be. They were designed to be appliquéd onto a background. The 8" compass can also be appliquéd, or it can be pieced into a circle drawn from the pattern.

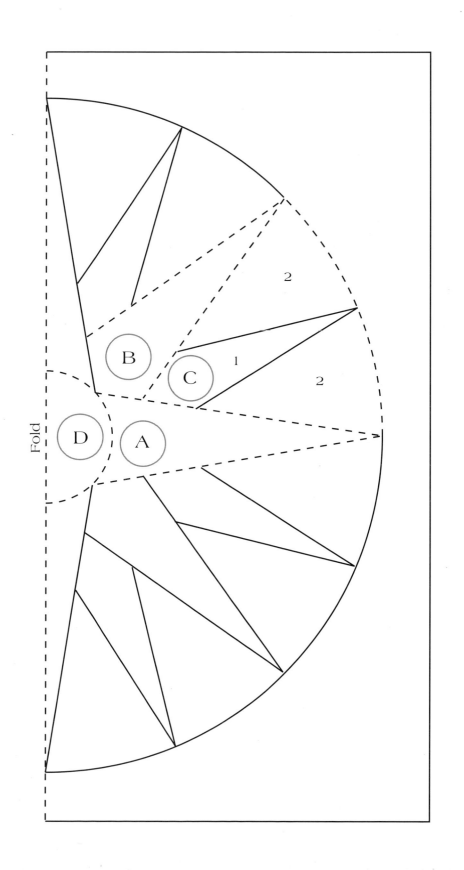

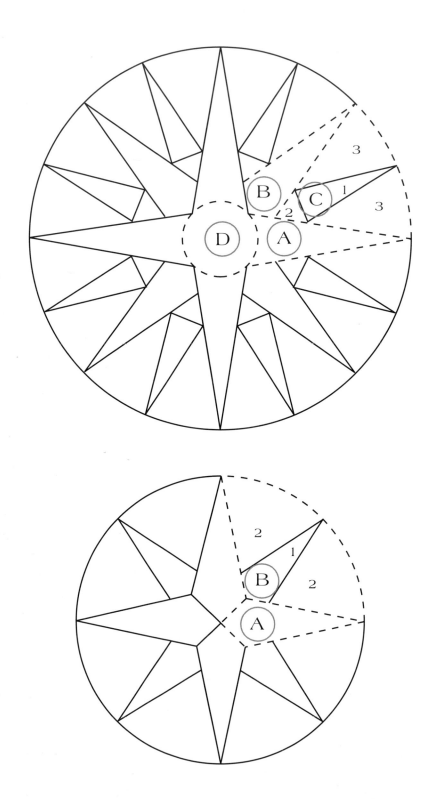

WAGON WHEELS

Block Plate 63

  Gallery Plates 14, 15, 16

Size: 16"

Segments: 25

Piecing techniques: *Under* pressed-
  piecing, conventional piecing,
  appliqué

Drafting category: Curve-based

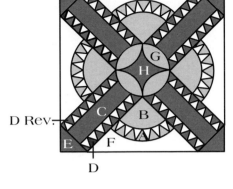

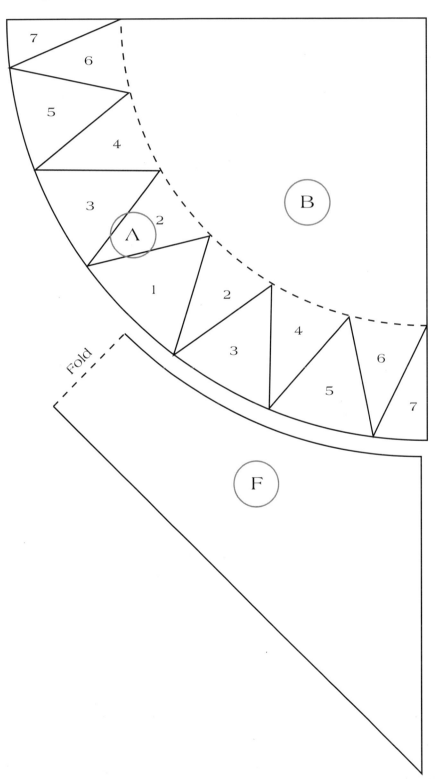

This pattern is a Kansas City Star pattern and is printed in sections that combine 12 press-pieced segments A and D, with 12 conventionally pieced segments B, C, E, and F. The center, H-G, is appliquéd. Draw one segment A and both segment Ds onto tracing paper. The two D segments are mirror images and it will be less confusing if they are drawn as one, and cut down the center later, see diagram. Needlepunch to produce the required number of foundations. This is an especially valuable marking technique for this block, because the rough side of the D foundations will indicate the right and left sides, avoiding confusion.

Press-piece the foundations, starting in the center and adding on each side. These are easily chain pieced. Trim the segments with a ¼" seam allowance. Cut B, C, and E, marking the sewing lines, and construct the block with conventional piecing. The center is appliquéd after the block is assembled.

PATTERNS
COMBINATION BLOCKS

49

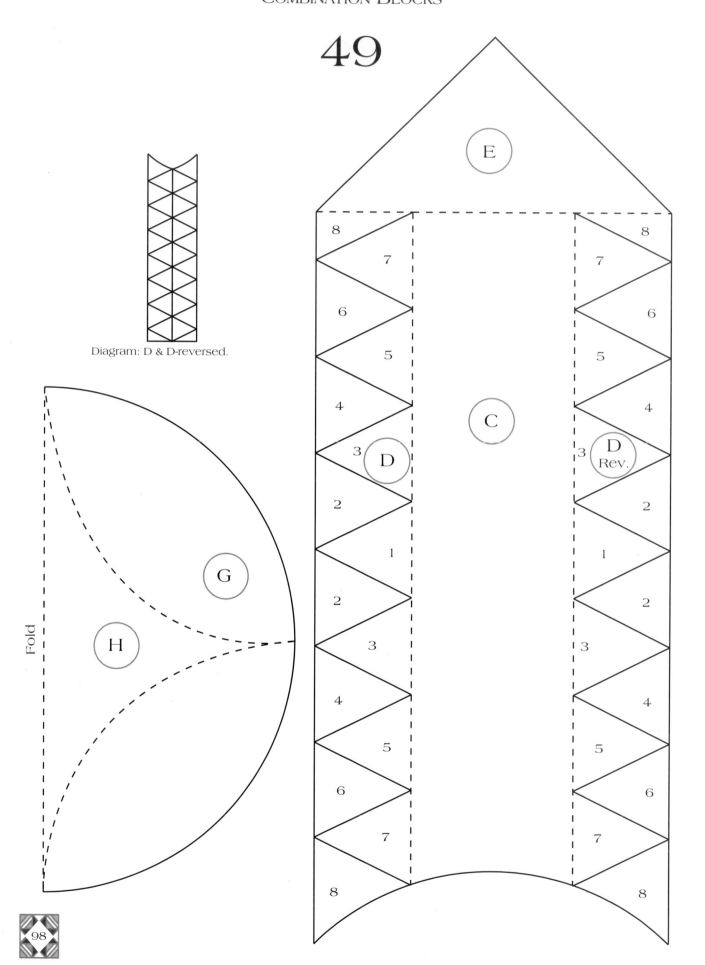

Diagram: D & D-reversed.

Fold

98

SUNFLOWER

Block Plates 66, 67

Size: 16"
Segments: 18
Piecing techniques: *Under* pressed-
   piecing, conventional piecing,
   appliqué
Drafting category: Mariner's Compass

50

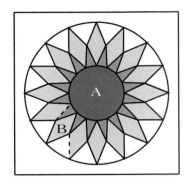

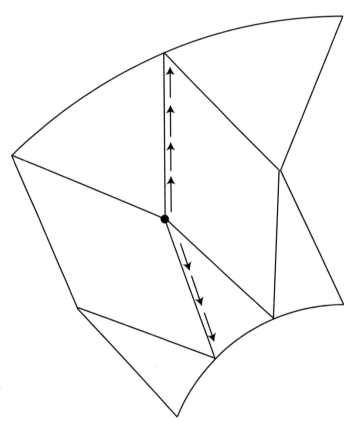

Diagram: two-step set-in.

This pattern is surprisingly easy to piece. One quarter of the pattern is printed. Trace the entire pattern onto freezer paper. The block has 16 identical press-pieced segments with shallow angles which are joined in a circle. Use rough-cut templates to cut fabric for these segments. Press-baste the fabric for the diamond area of the segment onto the shiny side of the freezer paper foundation with the tip of a hot iron to secure it. The segments can easily be press-pieced with chain piecing. It is important to press the completed segments firmly, from both the fabric and the paper sides, and trim the outer seam allowance to ¼".

Join the segments with a two step set-in process, see diagram. It is important to stitch outward from the inner angle in both directions, beginning the first stitch at the exact tip of the slim inner triangle to maintain its point. Appliqué the center onto the finished flower, which either can be pieced into an outer circle drawn from the edge of the pattern, or appliquéd onto a background.

Fold

Fold

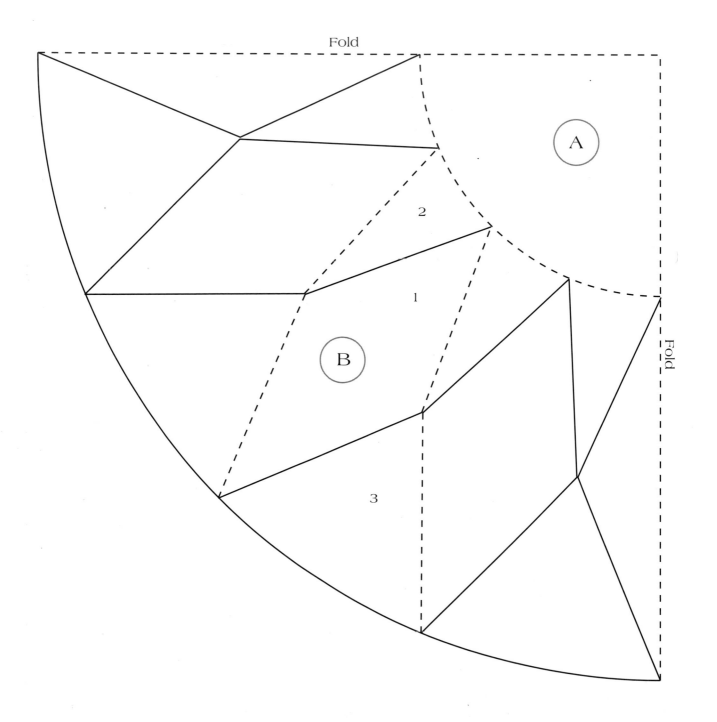

A

B

2

1

3

PATTERNS
Sheeted Triangle Grid for Blocks 51 & 52

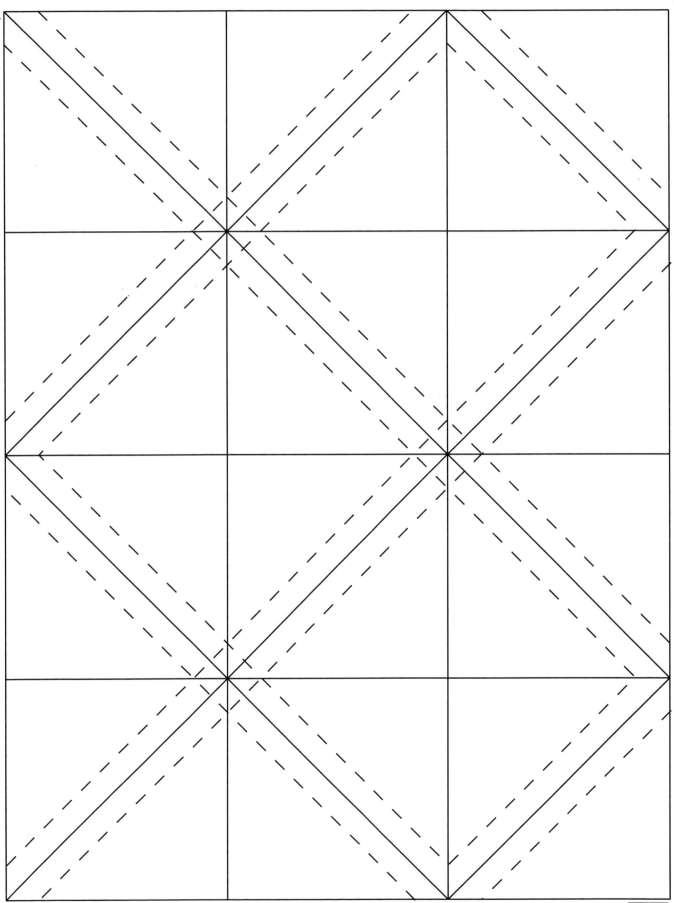

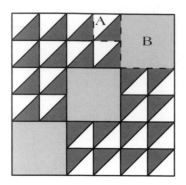

51

GOLDEN GATES

Block Plates 68, 69

Size: 8"

Segments: 27

Piecing techniques: Sheeted half-square triangles, single foundation piecing

Drafting category: Nine-Patch (36 grid)

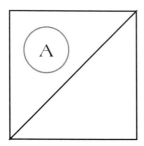

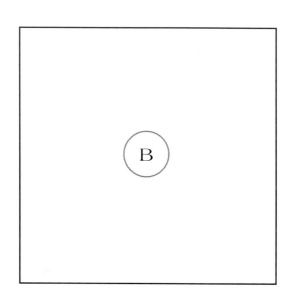

This block has two different segments, the half-square triangle unit A used 24 times and a large square B, repeated three times. Use freezer paper single foundations for the squares. Trace the grid on page 101 on typing paper to make the half-square triangles (Ref p. 19 – 20). It is important to draw the grid so that all the lines cross exactly at each intersection. You can draw the stitching lines that are ¼" on each side of the diagonal lines, or, if you have an accurate presser foot, use it to stitch these lines. Follow our grid pattern for the diagonal lines to avoid having stitches that will need to be removed across the corners of the squares. Use a smaller-than-usual stitch since you will be sewing through and removing thicker paper.

After stitching, press on the fabric side to set the stitches. Cut apart on all lines, remove the paper, and press open the squares toward the darker fabric. Assemble the block in rows, stitching accurately with an exact ¼" seam allowance.

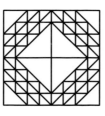

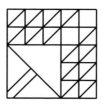

Ocean Wave   Pine Tree

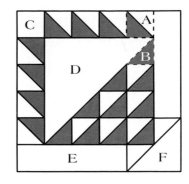

BASKET

Block Plate 70

Size 8"

Segments: 24

Piecing techniques: Sheeted half-square triangles, single foundation piecing, conventional piecing

Drafting category: Nine-Patch (36 grid)

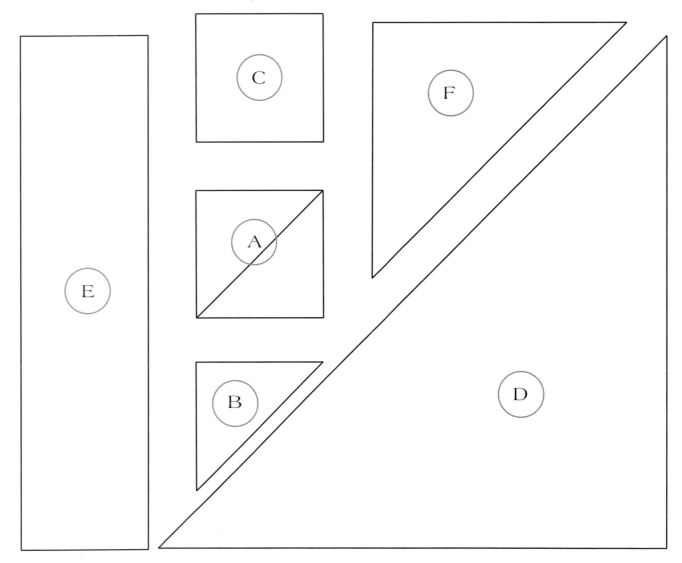

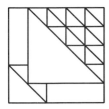

Chip Basket

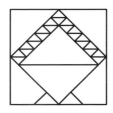

Fruit Basket

This block has 14 half-square triangle units A, 6 half-square triangles B, and four single templates. Trace the grid on page 101 on typing paper, and follow the directions on pages 19 – 20 to make half-square triangle units A. Using three squares the measurement of the grid squares, cut on the diagonals to form the 6 single half-square triangles B. Make single freezer paper foundations for C, D, E (2), and F. Assemble the basket in rows, sewing with a ¼" seam allowance.

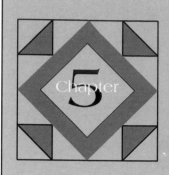

Chapter 5

THE QUILTS

We knew we had learned a lot about using foundations in the years since we introduced contemporary uses for foundation piecing. As we chose quilts for this book, we were reinforced in our conviction that foundation piecing is being widely used in exciting ways. Many of the quilts use blocks that are in the book, or similar ones, and this will help you see how the blocks can be used. All of the quilts were pieced on foundations in whole or in part.

Three of the quilts are group quilts. As a test of her belief that quilters of any level could piece blocks on foundations and have these blocks fit together, Dixie offered to teach a workshop to her guild. Quilters from novice to advanced skill levels were enrolled on the condition they would give her their "first-born" blocks of two different patterns for small quilts she could use as examples. Their enthusiam was more than she bargained for; she ended up with four lap-size or larger quilt tops. But her point was proven when all the blocks

fit together perfectly. WITH A LITTLE HELP...(Gallery Plate 1) uses Friendship Logs (Block Plate 4), and REMEMBER ME #1 (Gallery Plate 2) is made from the pattern of the same name (Block Plate 7).

As a result of this example, the show committee for the guild's biennial show became convinced the only way to piece blocks for a raffle quilt was with foundations. GULF STAR (Gallery Plate 3) is made from the pattern by the same name (Block Plate 33). The feat of fitting 99 pieced blocks together was made possible by using foundation piecing. A few blocks were unusable where the stitching was not confined to the sewing lines on the foundations or where the segments were carelessly joined, but this was a minor problem compared to the one that would have been faced with non-foundation pieced blocks.

Many of the quilts incorporate stars or star-based designs. Jane's STRING STAR (Gallery Plate 4) wallhanging was made using scraps of sueded cotton left over from other projects. The

eight-pointed stars were pieced on freezer paper single foundations, using her method of stitching the setting squares and triangles onto each diamond before assembling the star (Pattern 33, pg. 79-80). The pattern is one often found in quilts from the past, using scraps of strings and selvedges to create fabric from virtually nothing.

The string border was pieced on long strips of tracing paper, cut to fit the quilt. Both the star points and the borders were constructed using *top* pressed-piecing in random strips. The quilt is machine quilted.

Angela Bowen Helman's SHINING STAR quilt (Gallery Plate 18) was motivated by a string-piecing workshop through her guild. The workshop, combined with an overabundance of tropical fabric scraps and children suffering through chicken pox, resulted in her version of a traditional string-piecing set called "Hillbilly Star."

The tropical fabric scraps were pieced on a permanent foundation of unbleached muslin. Angie used a necktie-shaped paper pattern to block out a white space in the center of the block; when four blocks are sewn together, a star pattern results. "After piecing all the blocks, I wanted to emphasize the stars, and wasn't happy with sashing or alternate blocks. I eventually set the stars on point and did not fill in the remaining triangles with fabric." Angie machine quilted in the ditch on the tropical scraps and machine quilted with metallic silver thread in the stars, echoing the star shape.

Jane made the STAR SAMPLER (Gallery Plate 8) for a class in drafting and constructing stars. The blocks are simple and complex Nine-Patch, Four-Patch, eight-pointed, and diagonal designs. Most of the patterns are made using freezer paper and *under* pressed-piecing by itself or in combination with single foundations. A string or crazy star uses *top* pressed-piecing. The sashing stars were also foundation pieced. Several of the block patterns in the quilt are featured in the book.

OH MY STARS (Gallery Plate 5) is a teaching sampler designed by Lynn Graves. The quilt is composed of five different star patterns: Emily's Star (also known as Starry Path), St. Louis Star, State Fair Star, Pinwheel Star, and Mariner's Compass. Half Mariner's Compass blocks form the border.

Flat piping was used in the sashing. Starry Path (Block Plates 22, 23) and Mariner's Compass (Block Plates 64, 65, 66) are given in the pattern section as blocks for you to try. Lynn, the inventor of Little Foot™, produces many patterns for *top* pressed-piecing on foundations.

ASTRAL PROJECTION (Gallery Plate 6) by Ziek Gunn combines a 54-40 or Fight-type star (similar to the Gulf Star block) with a Trip Around the World set. The design is Ziek's own. She used foundations for the patches containing the points in the stars, printing the patterns on newsprint with her computer printer. These patches were trimmed and then combined with rotary-cut squares and conventional piecing to complete the block. The edges of the foundations provided an accurate sewing line for assembly. Ziek is a professional quiltmaker who uses foundations even in relatively simple designs for the speed and precision she can achieve.

STAR FANTASY (Gallery Plate 7) by Terry Northup was designed using Jeffrey Gutcheon's *Diamond Patchwork* and the 54-40 or Fight Star. The resulting skewed diamond star block is composed of smaller diamonds measuring less than one inch. She decided to use foundations and pieced the diamonds in three horizontal strips to form the blocks. She used single foundations for the body of the quilt, to

give stability as well as accuracy to the quilt top. The appliqué center was adapted from a photograph of her daughter.

Dixie's vest and her TWILIGHT TIME quilt, (Gallery Plates 10 and 13) both use the Dixie's Star block. The pattern resulted from a doodle she made, and since we have not found it in any of the pattern collections, we took the liberty of naming it. The vest blocks are colored like our sample (Block Plate 12) with multi-color stars formed when blocks are joined. Dixie believes that combining one pieced vest front with a plain quilted front is an example of the "less is more" concept that makes patchwork wearable.

The quilt combines hand-dyed and commercially dyed "atmospheric" fabrics and was an experiment to see if they could be used together. Cutting was the scary part. If it hadn't worked, a great deal of hand-dyed fabric would have been difficult to re-use in another pattern! The usual technique of marking color placement on the foundations was not practical with this quilt, which had to be composed in advance on the design wall. A single block was removed, laid out in the piecing order, pieced to the foundation, and replaced on the wall. Each row was pieced as the blocks in it were completed to avoid the possibility their positions would be switched.

RAVEN'S FOREST (Gallery Plate 9) is another doodle pattern. Dixie drafted the Grandpa's Pride block, a combination of two units (Block Plate 64) from a doodle her husband made. The pattern has been used to make quilts for their grandchildren, using different color arrangements to create individual quilts for each of them (Figures 5-1, 5-2). Dixie has more quilts designed from this pattern than she has (or is likely to have) grandchildren, so she is thinking of piecing for the next generation! All the quilts from this pattern were designed on the wall before piecing; only Raven's Forest was pieced on foundations. Using foundations speeded up the piecing and stabilized the edges of the units, making it much easier to match the points as the rows were joined.

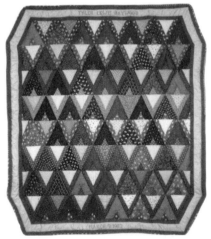

FIG. 5-1.
GRANDPA'S PRIDE I, Dixie Haywood, 1983.
Made for Tyler Lewis Haywood. 52" x 52"

Among the most difficult patterns to execute in fabric are those of the Mariner's Compass family. The MARINER'S COMPASS in red and black (Gallery Plate 19) was designed from a photograph of

FIG. 5-2. GRANDPA'S PRIDE II,
Dixie Haywood, 1988.
Made for Cedar Lewis Howard. 62" x 62".

an Amish quilt Jane saw in a magazine some years ago. She was impressed by the complexity of the pattern coupled with the simplicity created by using only two colors. She used three different black fabrics in the compasses, turning some of the fabrics to the wrong side to achieve the effect she wanted. One of the Mariner's Compass patterns we give (Block Plate 62) has the same built-in background circle effect as in this quilt.

The compasses are pieced on freezer paper, using *under* pressed-piecing and single foundations. The centers are hand appliquéd. The pieced compasses are set into the large background blocks by machine. The borders were pieced on long strips of freezer paper, measured to fit the sides of the quilt exactly.

Once the borders were sewn onto the quilt, before removing the foundations, Jane put stabilizing strips on the outside edges where the many seams could cause it to stretch and wobble; she in effect bound the quilt before quilting it.

The piece is hand quilted, using feathered wreath designs to reinforce the compass pattern.

STARS ABOVE (Gallery Plate 20) was Jane's entry into a Hoffman Challenge contest a few years ago. The fabric for the challenge was the dark sky fabric with stars and planets strewn across it. Jane made thirteen Mariner's Compasses, ranging in size from 3" to 7", in different fabrics using the colors and shades from the challenge fabric. She appliquéd these onto the background, placing them randomly. Patterns for three of the compasses are in this book. (Block Plates 61 & 62). The piece is hand quilted, using metallic thread for the star-shine lines, and dark blue for the remainder.

Linda Halpin used several sizes of Mariner's Compass designs to create her reversible BOG COAT (Gallery Plate 11). She drafted the patterns on large sheets of tracing paper, which served as her master pattern. After planning the color placement, she broke the compasses into segments, stitched fabric to the units, and joined them to make the large units. Linda wanted a particular line of the checked fabric to follow the outer edge of the compass so she cut additional tracing paper templates for those segments, positioned, and basted them to the fabric. She pinned these paper/fabric pieces to the larger tracing paper overlay, and joined the segments, removing the extra layer of paper. Linda discovered that by folding the paper back on itself and creasing it along the seamline, the paper seemed to be cut by the stitches and was easy to remove.

She says "The intrigue of incorporating foundation piecing into the construction of a bog coat is the flexibility it gave me to design two differing versions of the same compass shape for one garment...Using removable paper allowed me a firm foundation to build on, avoiding stretch and distortion, yet did not add any bulk to the completed garment."

Another pattern involving curves and many points was used for three of Dixie's quilts. ANNIVERSARY STAR, SUMMERTIME, and OLÉ (Gallery Plates 14, 15, and 16) are part of a series exploring the color yellow and the Wagon Wheels pattern (Block Plate 63). Varying tones, tints, and shades of yellow are used for different elements of the pattern in each quilt.

The quilts combine foundation segments and conventional piecing. Foundation piecing was crucial to the accuracy of the design, although the majority of the piecing was not done on foundations. All of the sawtooth portions of the quilt were *under* press-pieced on tracing paper, as were the long points on ANNIVERSARY STAR. The sawtooth elements shown in the pattern are those used for

SUMMERTIME and ANNIVERSARY STAR; they were refined after making OLÉ, which uses larger ones.

Karen Stone's INDIAN ORANGE PEEL (Gallery Plate 21) is a masterpiece of curves, points of all sizes, and colors. Karen combined a traditional Orange Peel design with elements from an orange antique Indian Wedding Ring quilt in the Pilgrim/Roy collection to create this quilt. She used *under* pressed-piecing, adding a fabric placement line to mark her seam allowances and help position the fabric. Her first quilt using foundations was a Pineapple design from our *Perfect Pineapples*, and she says, "paper foundations were a wonderful revelation to me – a major technical breakthrough. The details were taken care of automatically, the blocks all fit together, and the quilt was nice and flat."

Log Cabin designs are often pieced on foundations, which can be used to create innovative designs using this old favorite pattern. FIREFLIES (Gallery Plate 28) was stitched on tracing paper using *under* pressed-piecing and a corner based Log Cabin design. Jane used a packet of hand-dyed fabric and when she played with the blocks, rotating them, they created flashes of light like fireflies on a summer night. It is hand quilted in circles and rays to reinforce the design concept.

Kathy Sullivan's MINI COMPULSIVE LOG CABIN (Gallery Plate 27) is sewn on paper foundations using *under* pressed-piecing. This pattern allows an ordered look to the cotton scrap fabrics by using solid colored triangles to separate the light and dark strips. Each block in this small Sunshine and Shadow wallhanging measures 3¾". Kathy has constructed this pattern using many different colorations and sizes with blocks as small as 2". They were all worked on paper foundations to ensure the necessary accuracy.

Jane's vest (Gallery Plate 12) is made of handwoven Thai silk, using the Courthouse Steps variation of a Log Cabin pattern (Block Plate 1). The small blocks were *under* press-pieced on tracing paper foundations. The vest was constructed by string piecing strips along the sides of the blocks, using *top* pressed-piecing on a thin batting foundation. Using the same fabric in this design, which turns strips of fabric at right angles, gives a texture and design that changes with the play of light. The garment is simple, low-key, and elegant, making it wearable in a number of situations.

THE CHINESE QUILT (Fig 5-3) was purchased on the Great Wall in China for Jane by a friend. A child's quilt, it is designed to protect him from bad creatures such as spiders, snakes, and scorpions. What intrigued us was the

FIG. 5-3.
Chinese double-sided child's quilt with foundation-pieced Pineapple blocks on back

back of the quilt, a simple Pineapple design sewn on foundations. The fabric is mostly cottons of varying textures. The Chinese newspapers remain inside, and the print can be seen through some of the lighter fabrics.

Dare MacKellar's process of designing her FLYING PINEAPPLE TIDBITS (Gallery Plate 26) illustrates the fact that designing is a function which needs both inspiration and technique. The roots of this quilt started several years ago when Dare purchased an off-center Log Cabin wallhanging. This inspired her to draft an off-center block with the ends of some of the logs cut diagonally to give the illusion of birds flying about when the blocks were set together. That quilt never saw the cutting board when she realized how tedious it would be to cut and piece her design. When our first book, *Perfect Pineapples*, was published, she thought it might be interesting to see what off-center drafting would do to the basic Pineapple block – and "there before my eyes on the

drafting paper appeared those flying birds!" *Under* pressed-piecing removes the tedium from cutting and piecing, so this time she followed through and made the quilt.

The blocks were pieced on a fine cotton foundation, and marked with a hot-iron transfer. She made a colored and numbered paper template for each of the block repeats to make the piece mistake proof. Her comment about Pineapples echoes ours: "One could probably make nothing but Pineapples for the rest of one's quilting career and never have two that looked alike."

Our off-center Pineapple (Block Plates 10, 11) is not the same block that Dare used, but its design possibilities are equally as full of potential as she found in her pattern.

We have both worked with this pattern extensively and remain excited by its versatility. Jane is working on a series of Pineapple colorwash quilts. Using the strong diagonal design line in the pattern, she began to experiment with placing colors so a run of colors would wash across the quilt, from one corner to the opposite. CHROMA I (Gallery Plate 23) used only subtle tone-on-tone prints, in clear colors, beginning with red, and working through purple and blue to green. Jane had to overdye two of the thirteen fabrics to achieve exactly the right shade. She also used

the Pineapple block to create the background surrounding the large center design.

The blocks are pieced on tracing paper, using *under* press-piecing. The inner border is pieced on tracing paper, and uses all the fabrics in the quilt, sewn into 1" squares. The quilt is hand quilted in circles and lines reinforcing the patterns.

Two other quilts in the series use the same colorwash design concept with a pieced-in background. CHROMA II: BERRY-PATCH (Gallery Plate 24) uses solid color hand-dyed fabrics and has a hand-appliquéd vine border. The body of the quilt is machine quilted in arcs, and the border is hand quilted. CHROMA III: VINIFERA (Gallery Plate 25) is made with printed tone-on-tone fabrics which run from dark purple through blue, teal, and green. The inner border is made of hand appliquéd swags; it is entirely hand quilted.

CHROMA IV: CANYON (Gallery Plate 22) uses the same idea of a diagonal colorwash using the Pineapple pattern and hand-dyed sueded cotton fabrics. However, instead of piecing individual blocks with each color, Jane opted to run the colors across the quilt, in a shallow diagonal line, moving up and down along the strips of each consecutive Pineapple block. The blocks are separated with a ½" dark navy blue windowpane strip. Outline quilting around strips and borders is done by machine. The diagonal wavy lines are hand quilted.

Many of the quilts in the book are taken directly from traditional patterns. Gerry Winstead made THE PINE BURR (Gallery Plate 31) top after learning about using foundations for piecing difficult patterns. She drafted the block and pieced the center star figure entirely on tracing paper, using *under* pressed-piecing. She used a single foundation for the center curved piece and made a template for the large side triangles, using conventional piecing to set them into the star, forming a block. This graphic pattern is often not attempted, or if done, is not worked accurately due to the many small triangles and points. We include the pattern for this block in a 12" size (Block Plate 54) and in a slightly simplified version in an 8" size (Block Plate 53).

LULA'S QUILT II (Gallery Plate 30) was made by Barbara Elwell to replicate a full-sized quilt made by her grandmother. The pattern, Jack in the Pulpit (Block Plate 38), was divided into a center segment and four corners for *under* pressed-piecing. Barbara needle punched the corners on one stack of tracing paper and the centers on another to reproduce the foundations quickly and accurately. She learned to cut fabric patches oversize, to ensure adequate seam allowances and coverage of the pattern areas. Before assembling

the blocks, she drew midline registration marks on all the pieced segments to make the assembly placement accurate and easier.

SPIDER'S WEB (Gallery Plate 32) was made by Marion Roach Watchinski to replicate a quilt her mother-in-law's grandmother, Buena Vesta Evans Evans (her maiden and married names were the same) made around the turn of the century in Shelby County, Illinois. The original quilt is quite ripply and wavy, and Marion was certain she could eliminate the ripples and waves with foundation methods.

Her first step was to draft the main block and its ajoining whole sashing. Marion discovered the block had to be 15¾" in order to work and that the "square" in the center of the whole sashing was really a short, stubby diamond and not a square at all. The other units making up the design are a half-sash, a half-block, and a corner. All five units were traced onto tracing paper and then photocopied. The photocopies were used as foundations for the Flying Geese piecing. The diamond shapes for the 8-pointed stars were cut as for conventional hand piecing, and sewn to the ends of the sashing units. The half blocks, whole blocks, and corners had larger rotary-cut muslin triangles added accordingly. Finally, the sashings and block units were joined. Marion says, "This quilt top was quite

challenging and incorporated many different quilting techniques. It may not be for the beginning foundation piecer, but the outcome was well worth the effort. I think great-grandma Evans would be proud!"

Eileen Gudmundson's OCEAN WAVES (Fig. 5-4) in her signature achromatic coloration was made with the hybrid sheeted triangle method. She initially learned this faster method in a guild work party. When she tried to photocopy a copy of a copy of the half-square triangle sheet, she discovered the triangles were distorted in the process. Copying from the original sheet corrected the problem.

FIG. 5-4. OCEAN WAVES,
Eileen Gudmunsdon, Lillian, AL, 1993.
61½" x 61½".

Joyce Schneider uses foundations in yet another way, combining small or miniature blocks to form large quilt-sized blocks. SUNDAY ON THE BAY (Gallery Plate 29) was designed for the block-of-the-month program at her local quilt shop. Each of the twelve blocks is a different sailboat set either singly or with the pieced miniatures used as patches to form a large traditional block. Such favorites as Variable Star, Jacob's Ladder (which she renamed Jacob's Regatta with its flotilla of boats), and Flock of Geese are the basis for these blocks which make up a queen-sized quilt. She floated the blocks with sashing and sailboat corner-stones, adding a sawtooth border. This is a practical and creative way to use miniature blocks in a larger quilt.

Quiltmakers are using foundations to build on and move out from traditional patterns. The advantage of being able to draw and design directly on a foundation, on which you will then piece, is both efficient and effective.

ELECTRIC STAR (Gallery Plate 17), made from the pattern of the same name (Block Plate 19), was designed on a computer using the Electric Quilt™ program. Dixie wanted to make a planned crazy quilt for *Ties, Ties, Ties* by Janet Elwin. Playing with arrangements of the block led to the 4-block star image; secondary images emerged as the star blocks were joined. The design possibilities of the small quilt she made from ties inspired Dixie to make this larger version with cotton fabrics. It is pieced using *under* pressed-piecing to maintain the design lines. The inside border was pieced on parallelogram-shaped foundations the size of the blocks. The next two borders were pieced on freezer paper. The stars in the border were pieced using single freezer paper founda-

tions and then appliquéd in place.

Dixie's crazy quilts, CRAZY CRACKER (Figure 5-5) and SOHO SUNDAY (Gallery Plate 35) use *top* pressed-piecing. CRAZY CRACKER is derived from the Cracker block (Block Plate 2) with the straight lines of the center bars changed to curves. This quilt was drawn full size on tracing paper, which was cut into separate foundations, pieced and sewn together. While the design of the quilt went unchanged, the color placement did not. Crazy quilting with multiple fabrics, even of the same colors, can turn out differently than expected. Fortunately, when Dixie changed the color placement, she was able to recycle crazy quilted sections on one foundation shape by pinning them to another shape and continuing the piecing.

FIG. 5-5. CRAZY CRACKER,
Dixie Haywood, 1993. 33" x 33".

SOHO SUNDAY is based on a small watercolor by Kandinsky, seen in the Soho branch of the Solomon R. Guggenheim Museum in New York City. The grid and the graphics of the original are given texture by the use of same-fabric

crazy quilting in the grid sections. A postcard of the watercolor was measured and the measurements multiplied to enlarge the scale. The full-sized grid was drawn onto tracing paper. Each section was coded for location and color on the back of the drawing. When the section was *top* pressed-pieced, the coding remained visible on the back of the section as a guide for the construction. Each section was cut from the layout as it was pieced.

While most of the quilt was *top* press-pieced, the black graphic detail, drawn on the back of the sections, was largely *under* press-pieced. Because of the geometry involved, some of the detail had to be drawn on a separate foundation, pieced, and then pieced onto the main foundation. The thin black sashing was added during the construction with conventional piecing. The quilt is machine quilted in the ditch to emphasize the texture of the crazy quilting.

Susan Brown made XIAOPING'S WEDDING WINDOW (Gallery Plate 33) from a design she found in a stained glass window at the church where a friend was being married. She drew the design on her computer and printed templates for foundation piecing on freezer paper and tracing paper (Figure 5-6).

Susan crazy pieced on each pie-shaped stained glass shape, then top stitched silk ribbon and bias strips onto the sections creating

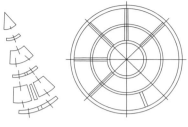

FIG. 5-6.

"leading." Large leading arcs were also printed as single foundation templates on freezer paper. She assembled the window into eight pie-shaped pieces and added the "leading" shapes, using registration marks printed on each foundation to position them precisely. They were trimmed for accuracy, and combined to form the quilt top. The fabrics are all cottons. The quilting is by machine, outlining the shapes and the leading.

PINWHEEL PIZAZZ (Gallery Plate 34) was made by Martha Smith after a workshop with Doreen Speckman. It is an original design formed by rotating an irregularly divided right triangle, and then rotating the resulting square. She designed and colored the quilt on her computer, then printed all the foundations on tracing paper.

The quilt is constructed of silk douppioni, Thai silk, and lamés. Martha says foundations were necessary to control the difficult fabric and to ensure accurate piecing of the silk. Although she backed the silks and lamés with fusible knit to increase their stability, they were slippery and some of them had a distinct directional weave which had to be controlled.

AFTER THE STORM (Gallery Plate 36) by Eileen Sullivan was constructed with *under* pressed-piecing on freezer paper foundations. After a few thumbnail sketches to work out the layout, each section was drawn full size on freezer paper starting with the sand, sea grass, and water. Using *under* pressed-piecing, the quilt was sewn in sections, which were joined to each other in logical order. When necessary, one section was appliquéd to another. Appliqué was used for the foreground sea shells. The top and right hand borders were the last to be designed and are a variation of Storm at Sea. Eileen says the foundation technique afforded her great freedom in designing, and also simplified the piecing which would have been impossible with conventional techniques. The back of the quilt is pieced with Storm at Sea blocks drafted in a diminishing perspective, also pieced on foundations.

Cynthia England made PIECE AND QUIET (Gallery Plate 37) entirely on single foundations using freezer paper. The quilt contains over 7,000 pieces of fabric in the quilt. She began with a photograph which she enlarged and drew on freezer paper. After choosing colors and fabrics, she made a color chart showing all of her fabric choices. Many of the fabrics were used on both sides to create depth and shading. The master pattern was coded for color, major sections/subsections, and piecing order, with registration

marks on seams that needed to be matched. The freezer paper pattern was copied as a reference; after copying, it was cut apart.

Working by sections, Cynthia ironed the freezer paper pieces onto the *right* side of the fabrics. After cutting out the fabric pieces with seam allowances added, she joined them, matching the freezer paper edges, not the seam allowances. She folded back the seam allowance to check that the edges of the papers were aligned and creased the fabric to indicate the stitching line. After stitching, if the seam was slightly off the edge of the freezer paper, she repositioned it by pressing. "The best thing about this technique is that it is extremely forgiving. Making this quilt was just like constructing a jigsaw puzzle except that I knew exactly where each piece went, and like a jigsaw puzzle, it was very addicting. The quilt literally made itself."

The Gallery bears out our belief that foundation work is widespread and shows that foundations are valuable whether you are making traditional or innovative quilts in simple or complex designs. Understanding and use of foundation techniques are still in the growing and learning stage and we expect them to produce even more exciting quilts. We hope the information contained in this book as well as the patterns and quilts will inspire you to explore these and other designs that can be made easier by the use of foundations.

111

GALLERY

PLATE 1
WITH A LITTLE HELP . . .
Dixie Haywood, 1994. 56" x 56".
Blocks made by members of the
Pensacola Quilters' Guild.

PLATE 2
REMEMBER ME #1
Dixie Haywood, 1994. 62" x
62". Blocks made by members
of the Pensacola Quilters' Guild.

GALLERY

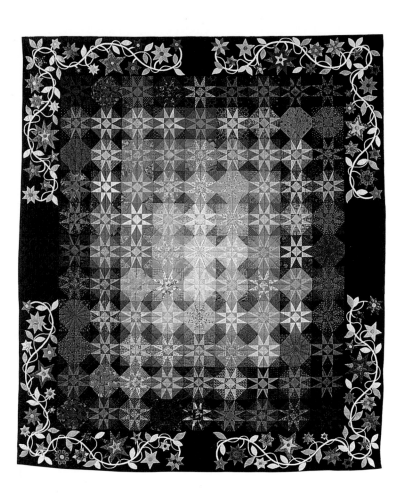

PLATE 3
GULF STAR
Pensacola Quilters' Guild, 1995.
92" x 108". From the collection of
Mary J. Richardson, Pensacola, FL.

PLATE 4
STRING STAR
Jane Hall, 1994. 30" x 38".

GALLERY

PLATE 5
OH MY STARS
Lynn Graves, Albuquerque, NM, 1995. 47" x 47". Pieced by Marion Wolpert and quilted by Barb Sawyer.

PLATE 6
ASTRAL PROJECTION
Ziek Gunn, Wilmington, NC, 1994. Quilted by Sherry Rhodes. From the collection of Martha Pierce Royal.

GALLERY

PLATE 7
STAR FANTASY
Terry Northup, Pensacola, FL, 1995.
36" x 40".

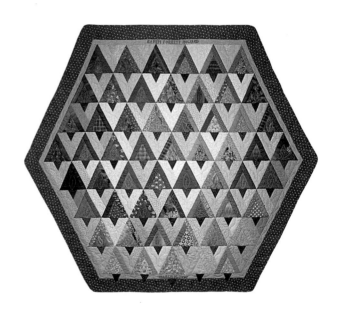

PLATE 9
RAVEN'S FOREST
Dixie Haywood, 1994. 62" x 56".
Made for Raven Forrest Howard.
Photo courtesy of the artist.

PLATE 8
STAR SAMPLER
Jane Hall, 1994. 27" x 40".

GALLERY

PLATE 12
SILK VEST
Jane Hall, 1995.

PLATE 10
VEST
Dixie Haywood, 1993.

PLATE 11
BOG COAT (Reversible)
Linda Halpin, Reedsburg, WI, 1995.
Construction information for this garment is in *Beyond the Bog Coat*. See Bibliography.

GALLERY

PLATE 13
TWILIGHT TIME
Dixie Haywood, 1995. 56" x 71".

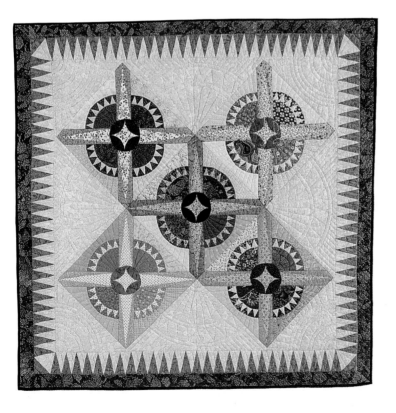

PLATE 14
ANNIVERSARY STAR
Dixie Haywood, 1994. 47" x 47".

GALLERY

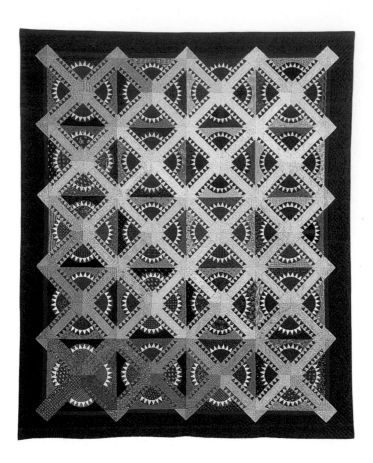

PLATE 15
SUMMERTIME
Dixie Haywood, 1994. 76" x 91".

PLATE 16
OLÉ
Dixie Haywood, 1993. 58" x 58".

GALLERY

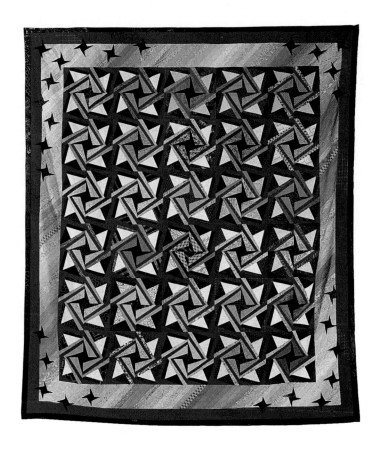

PLATE 17
ELECTRIC STAR
Dixie Haywood, 1996. 80" x 94".

PLATE 18
SHINING STAR
Angela Bowen Helman,
Pensacola, FL, 1993. 44" x 44".
From the collection of
Tami Rose.

GALLERY

PLATE 19
MARINER'S COMPASS
Jane Hall, 1995. 65" x 65".

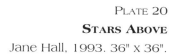

PLATE 20
STARS ABOVE
Jane Hall, 1993. 36" x 36".

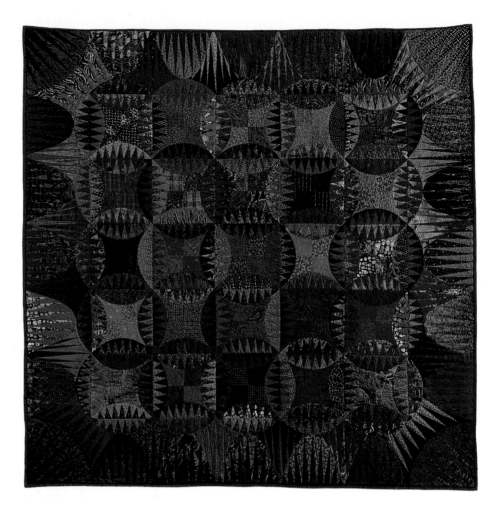

PLATE 21
INDIAN ORANGE PEEL
Karen Stone, Dallas, TX, 1994.
63" x 63".

PLATE 22
CHROMA IV: CANYON
Jane Hall, 1994. 46" x 46".

PLATE 23
CHROMA I
Jane Hall, 1993. 56" x 56". This quilt was given by the city
of Durham, NC, to its sister city, Toyama, Japan.
Photo courtesy of *Quilter's Newsletter Magazine*.

PLATE 24
CHROMA II: BERRYPATCH
Jane Hall, 1993. 36" x 36".

PLATE 25
CHROMA III: VINIFERA
Jane Hall, 1994. 56" x 56".

GALLERY

PLATE 26
FLYING PINEAPPLE TIDBITS
Dare C. MacKellar, Pensacola, FL,
1993. 29" x 29".

PLATE 27
MINI COMPULSIVE LOG CABIN
Kathy Sullivan, Raleigh, NC, 1986. 20" x 20".

PLATE 28
FIREFLIES
Jane Hall, 1994. 30" x 30".

GALLERY

PLATE 29
SUNDAY ON THE BAY
Joyce Schneider, Catonsville, MD,
1994. 88" x 109". Quilted by Forest
Morrison.

PLATE 30
LULA'S QUILT II
Barbara Elwell, Ashburn, VA,
1994. 54" x 43".

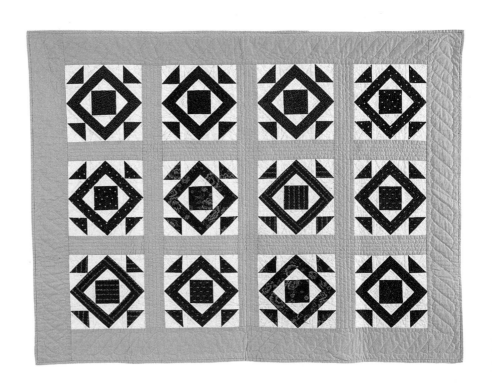

GALLERY

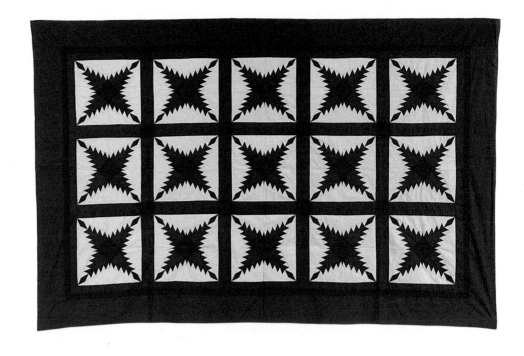

PLATE 31
THE PINE BURR
Gerry Winstead,
Raleigh, NC. 1994.
82" x 66".

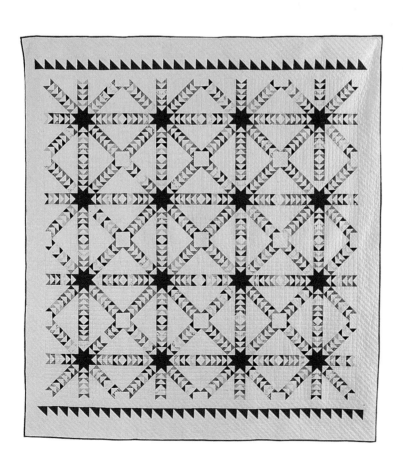

PLATE 32
SPIDER'S WEB
Marion Roach Watchinski, Overland
Park, KS, 1995. 84" x 93".

PLATE 33

XIAOPING'S WEDDING WINDOW

Susan Brown, Durham, NC, 1993.
32" diameter.

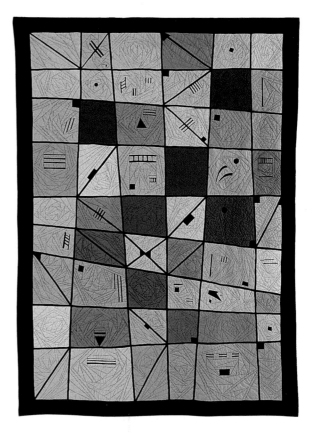

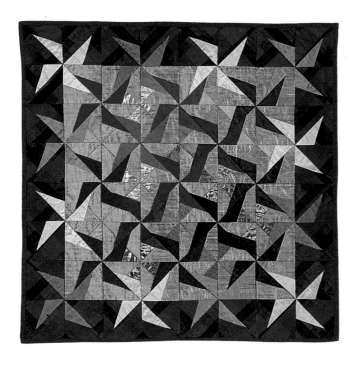

PLATE 35

SOHO SUNDAY

Dixie Haywood, 1995. 50" x 67".

PLATE 34

PINWHEEL PIZAZZ

Martha Smith, Chapel Hill, NC, 1994. 32" x 32".

GALLERY

PLATE 36
AFTER THE STORM
Eileen Sullivan, Alpharetta, GA,
1993. 69" x 79".

PLATE 37
PIECE AND QUIET
Cynthia England, Houston, TX, 1993.
80" x 64".

APPENDIX A
Troubleshooting

• **MY BLOCK DOESN'T LIE FLAT AFTER THE FOUNDATIONS ARE REMOVED.**

Too long a stitch or careless pressing can cause this problem. Stitch with a shorter stitch so it will not be loosened or distorted by removal of the foundation, and press each piece as it is sewn so it is taut against the foundation.

• **MY BLOCK DOESN'T LIE FLAT WHEN I PIECE SEGMENTS TOGETHER.**

Did you trace the block accurately? Did you stitch it accurately? Did you hold the fabric firmly and taut on the edges of the segments by pinning or basting as you stitched them together? Like any piecing, the final block can be distorted when the stitching is inaccurate.

• **I HAVE A DIFFICULT TIME GETTING SHARP POINTS AT THE EDGES OF MY BLOCK.**

Several techniques can be used to firm up a point at the edge of a block. Stitch across the seam allowance on the second seam of a point rather than starting or ending the stitching just beyond the point. You can stabilize the edge of a block that has the seam allowance added to the outside edge of the foundation by basting in the seam allowance. Freezer paper foundations are useful for patterns with points at the edge of the block, since the points will be adhered to the paper. Another trick is to aim your sewing machine needle so the lines forming a point cross at exactly the right spot to create a sharp point.

• **WHY, WHEN I HAVE SEWN ON THE LINE, ARE THE MATCHING POINTS SOMETIMES SLIGHTLY OFF?**

Did you position and pin the match points so they were exactly together? Did you stitch directly on the line? Did you press the preceding strip open without any fold?

• **THE PATCH DOESN'T COVER THE AREA IT'S SUPPOSED TO.**

Rough cut the fabric with a larger seam allowance, and lay the patch in position on top of the area to be sure it is cut large enough and aligned correctly before turning it over and stitching. Did you trim the previously sewn seam allowance to ¼" to allow proper positioning of the new piece? If the seam allowance is not trimmed, the next piece added will have too large a seam, causing it to fall short when it is opened.

• **MY PATCHES FOLD BACK WHEN I PUT THE FOUNDATION UNDER THE PRESSER FOOT OF THE MACHINE FOR UNDER PRESSED-PIECING.**

Put an anchoring pin at the top of the piece that will push under the feed dogs on the foundation side, removing it when the foundation is positioned for sewing if necessary. For a long strip, pin at each end to avoid shifting as it is sewn.

• **IS IT REALLY ESSENTIAL TO PIN?**

For accuracy, pressed-piecing depends on having the previous strip held flat and securely to the foundation. Whether you are using *top* or *under* pressed-piecing, pinning will keep the presser foot from moving the base strip. With single foundation piecing, pinning is the only way to ensure that the edges of the foundations are matched along the entire seamline.

APPENDIX A
Troubleshooting

• **CAN I FINGER PRESS?**

See Problem #1. It is not as effective as a hot iron. However, if you find it necessary to finger press, do so firmly. Then pin the fabric flat, close to the seam, to hold it taut against the foundation.

• **WHY CAN'T I TRIM ALL THE SEAMS AT ONCE AFTER THE BLOCK IS COMPLETED?**

In the pressed-piecing process, each subsequent row of stitches crosses and entraps the seam allowances from the previously sewn seams. If there is excess fabric, it cannot be removed easily.

• **WHEN I'M PIECING A BLOCK IN SEGMENTS, SOMETIMES ONE IS BACKWARDS. WHAT HAPPENED?**

When using foundations of transparent materials, the stitching lines are visible from both sides and it is easy to turn one over and piece on the wrong side. This is not a problem unless it is an asymmetrical piece. You can avoid this by getting in the habit of marking "up" on each segment before cutting the block apart.

• **THE FREEZER PAPER DOESN'T STAY ON THE FABRIC WHEN I'M USING SINGLE FOUNDATIONS.**

This can be a problem, especially when manipulating the foundations for set-in seams. You can either re-press and pin the foundations if they loosen, or machine baste across or around them before you start to piece.

• **ISN'T IT FASTER TO PHOTOCOPY FOUNDATIONS RATHER THAN TRACING OR NEEDLE PUNCHING?**

Not in the long run. All copies distort, usually in one direction only. The precision you gain by using foundation piecing is negated when lines at the edges of the foundations don't match.

APPENDIX B
Bibliography

BEYER, JINNY. *Patchwork Patterns*. McLean, VA: EPM Publications, Inc, 1979.

BOYLES, MARGARET. *Miniature Quilts*. Des Moines, IA: Meredith Press, 1995.

BRACKMAN, BARBARA. *An Encyclopedia of Pieced Quilt Patterns*. Paducah, KY: American Quilter's Society, 1993.

CRAIG, SHARYN SQUIER. *Drafting Plus*. Montrose, PA: Chitra Publications, 1994.

DOAK, CAROL. *Easy Machine Paper Piecing*. Bothell, WA: That Patchwork Place, 1994.

_____. *Easy Reversible Vests*. Bothell, WA: That Patchwork Place, 1995.

DODDS, DOROTHY AND ANNE DUTTON. *Triangles on a Roll*. Tempe, AZ: Quilters' Ranch Inc., 1995.

ELWIN, JANET B. *Ties, Ties, Ties*. Paducah, KY: American Quilter's Society, 1996.

GRAVES, LYNN. *The Frame Game*. Albuquerque, NM: Little Foot Press, 1994.

GREENBERG, LESLIE-CLAIRE. *Sewing on the Line*. Bothell, WA: That Patchwork Place, 1993.

HALGRIMSON, JAN. *Scraps Can Be Beautiful*. Edmonds, WA: Weaver-Finch Publications, 1979.

HALL, JANE AND DIXIE HAYWOOD. *Perfect Pineapples*. Martinez, CA: C & T Publishing, 1989.

_____. *Precision Pieced Quilts Using the Foundation Method*. Radnor, PA: Chilton Book Company, 1992.

HAYWOOD, DIXIE. *Crazy Quilting Patchwork*. New York: Dover Publications, Inc.1986.

_____. *Quick-and-Easy Crazy Patchwork*. New York: Dover Publications, Inc., 1992.

HALPIN, LINDA. *Beyond the Bog Coat*. Columbia Cross Roads, PA: RCW Publishing Co., 1993.

HERLAN, TESS. *Patterns for Paper Piecing*. Redmond, WA: Paper Pieces, 1990.

LEMAN, BONNIE AND JUDY MARTIN. *Log Cabin Quilts, New Edition*. Wheat Ridge, CO: Leman Publications Inc., 1992.

MATHIESON, JUDY. *Mariner's Compass Quilts: New Directions*. Martinez, CA: C & T Publishing, 1995.

REHMEL, JUDY. *Key to 1000 Quilt Patterns*. Vol. 1, 2, 3. Richmond, IN: Self-published, 1978, 1979, 1980.

ROSINTOSKI, ELLEN. *Marvelous Mini Quilts for Foundation Piecing*. San Marcos, CA: American School of Needlework, 1994.

_____. *Iron-on Transfers for Foundation Piecing*. San Marcos, CA: American School of Needlework, 1994.

ROZMYN, MIA. *Freedom in Design*. Bothell, WA: That Patchwork Place, 1995.

SHIRER, MARIE AND BARBARA BRACKMAN. *Creature Comforts*. Lombard, IL: Wallace-Homestead, 1986. No longer in print.

APPENDIX C
Resource List

THE FOLLOWING COMPANIES HAVE PRODUCTS FOR FOUNDATION PIECING. PLEASE ENCLOSE A SELF-ADDRESSED STAMPED ENVELOPE WHEN INQUIRING.

AROUND THE BLOCK
1617 Ashby
Berkeley, CA 94703
(e-mail: ladye jan @ aol.com)
        Foundation piecing quarterly newsletter; patterns.

BOLINES AT INDIAN CREEK
R.R. 1, Box 315
Towanda, IL 61776
        Multi-use stamp for different blocks.

BONESTEEL'S HARDWARE AND QUILT CORNER
150 White Street
Hendersonville, NC 28739
        "Grid-Grip" gridded freezer paper; paper foundations for Pineapple blocks.

COTTONWOOD
P. O. Box 302
Palmyra, VA 22963
        Stamped fabric foundations, transfer patterns for miniature blocks.

THE DESIGNERS WORKSHOP (EILEEN SULLIVAN)
10495 Oxford Mill Circle
Alpharetta, GA 30202
        Patterns for original designs using freezer paper foundations.

EILEEN'S DESIGN STUDIO
4503 Bacon School Road
St. Joseph, MI 49085
        Muslin and paper foundations for miniature blocks.

ENGLAND DESIGN STUDIOS (CYNTHIA ENGLAND)
803 Voyager
Houston, TX 77062
        Patterns for original designs using freezer paper foundations.

MARY GOLDEN
Box 333
New Hampton, NY 13256
        Patterns and paper foundations for traditional blocks.

THE GOLDEN UNICORN, INC. (JOYCE SCHNEIDER)
106 Shady Nook Avenue
Catonsville, MD 21228
        Foundation patterns for miniature and full-sized blocks and quilts.

GRANNY NANNY'S
7521 Richmond Road
Williamsburg, VA 23188
        Pattern book, stamps, patterns, fabric, paper foundations for miniatures.

GRAPHIC IMPRESSIONS
1741 Masters Lane
Lexington, KY 40515
        Easy-Tear™ removeable foundation material; stencils.

BRENDA GROELZ
308 West HWT 34
Phillips, NE 68865
        Paper foundations for miniature blocks.

HAHNER/GRIFFIN STUDIOS
P.O. Box 178
Fanwood, NJ 07023
        Paper foundations for traditional blocks.

HALL/HAYWOOD, c/o JANE HALL
200 Transylvania Avenue
Raleigh, NC 27609
        Perfect Pineapples book; foundation paper patterns for traditional and off-center pineapple designs.

LYNDA LEE'S FOUNDATION MINIATURES
P.O. Box 249
Luray, VA 22835
        Muslin foundations for miniature blocks.

SHIRLEY LIBY
812 W. Cromer
Muncie, IN 47303
        Self-published books of foundation patterns for miniature blocks.

LITTLE FOOT, LTD. (LYNN GRAVES)
605 Bledsoe NW
Albuquerque, NM 87107
        Little Foot™ for ¼" seam; paper foundations for traditional *top* pressed-pieced blocks; Pineapple design book.

NORTHERN STAR
P.O. Box 409, Rt 55
Kauneonga Lake, NY 12749
        Foundation pattern for Mariner's Compass.

APPENDIX C
Resource List

PAPER PIECES
P.O. Box 2931
Redmond, WA 98073
Papers and book for English piecing.

PATCHWORK PLUS
2403 Silver Holly Lane
Richardson, TX 75082
Paper foundations for miniature blocks and borders.

QUILT ARTS
4114 Minstell Lane
Fairfax, VA 22033
Stamps for marking foundations for miniature blocks.

QUILT BY NUMBER
14 Chestnut Hill
Warren, NJ 07059
Foundations for miniature blocks.

QUILT DIRECTIONS
330 S. Ellison Lane
Waynesboro, VA 22980
Foundation patterns for miniature and full-sized traditional and original blocks; snowflakes.

THE QUILTED LADY (JUNE RYKER)
1464 South Ward Street
Lakewood, CO 80228
Innovative Log Cabin patterns using foundations with *top* pressed-piecing.

THE QUILTED RIBBON
P.O. Box 811
Derby, KS 67037
Foundations for Prairie Points; curved patterns.

QUILTER'S RANCH (DOROTHY DODDS, ANNE DUTTON)
107 E. Baseline Road
Tempe, AZ 85283
Half- and quarter-square triangle grids in rolls; triangle design book.

THE QUILTING DRONE
11 McKinley Street
Middletown, OH 45042
Self-published books of miniature foundation piecing patterns.

BONNIE JEAN ROSENBAUM
3513 Smith SE
Albuquerque, NM
Paper foundations for miniature blocks.

SCS DESIGNS (SONJA SHOGREN)
1815 Falls Church Road
Raleigh, NC 27609
Paper patterns for ultra-miniature Log Cabin designs.

SHIMP PERSONALIZED PUBLICATION SERVICES, INC.
4410 N. Rancho Dr., # 165
Las Vegas, NV 89130
Half and quarter-square triangle paper in tablets.

SMALL PATCHES
12715 Warwick Boulevard
Newport News, VA 23606
Stamps for marking foundations for miniature blocks.

THE STENCIL COMPANY
P.O. 1218
Williamsville, NY 14221
Plastic stencils for marking designs on foundations.

KAREN L. STONE DESIGNS
5418 Mc Commas Blvd.
Dallas, Tx 75206
Paper foundation patterns for traditional and innovative quilts.

THEE AND ME
220 Timberlane
South Bend, IN 46615
Stamps and muslin foundations for miniature blocks and borders.

THOROUGHLY MODERN MINIS
P.O. Box 925
Carpinteria, CA 93014
Stamps and design instructions for miniature blocks and quilts.

THROUGH THE SCREEN DOOR
4215 Avenue G
Kearney, NE 68847
Foundation pattern for sampler quilt of full-sized blocks.

TONI'S TREASURES
480 N. 3rd W.
Rigby, ID 83442
Muslin foundations for miniature and full-size blocks.

ZIPPY DESIGNS
RFD 1, Box 187M
Newport, VA 24128
(e-mail:ets@vt.edu)
Paper foundation patterns for quilts and wallhangings. Foundation piecing bi-montly newsletter.

GENERAL INDEX

BLOCK INDEX

Numbers in **bold** indicate a photo.

QUILTS & QUILTMAKERS INDEX

Numbers in **bold** indicate a photo.

AQS BOOKS ON QUILTS

This is only a partial listing of the books on quilts that are available from the American Quilter's Soceity. AQS books are known the world over for their timely topics, clear writing, beautiful color photographs, and accurate illustrations and patterns. Most of the following books are available from your local bookseller, quilt shop, or public library. If you are unable to locate certain titles in your area, you may order by mail from the AMERICAN QUILTER'S SOCIETY, P.O. Box 3290, Paducah, KY 42002-3290. Customers with Visa or MasterCard may phone in orders from 7:00–4:00 CST, Monday–Friday, Toll Free 1-800-626-5420. Add $2.00 for postage for the first book ordered and $0.40 for each additional book. Include item number, title, and price when ordering. Allow 14 to 21 days for delivery.